OUR MISSION IN CHRIST

BECOMING PEOPLE WHO WILL
CHANGE THE WORLD

ANDY ZIESEMER

Copyright © 2020 by A Jesus Mission Publishing LLC
Written by Andrew (Andy) Ziesemer

Scripture quotations marked CSB have been taken from the Christian Standard Bible®, Copyright © 2017 by Holman Bible Publishers. Used by permission. Christian Standard Bible® and CSB® are federally registered trademarks of Holman Bible Publishers. Any scripture references from other translations are notated where they occur.

All rights reserved. No part of this publication may be reproduced, distributed, or transmitted in any form or by any means, including photocopying, recording, or other electronic or mechanical methods, without the prior written permission of the publisher, except in the case of brief quotations embodied in critical reviews and certain other noncommercial uses permitted by copyright law. For permission requests, write to the publisher, addressed "Attention: Use Permissions" at the address below.

ISBN: 978-1-7359122-0-2 (Paperback)
ISBN: 978-1-7359122-1-9 (EPUB)

Edited by Kara N Young, Alissa Larsen, Jiross Lakey, and Diana Westfall
Internal page design and typesetting by Jiross Lakey
Cover design and digital assets created by KOER Media, www.koermedia.com
Printed by: AJM Publishing LLC
We make things that Unite the Mission, Equip the Found, and Find the Lost.

Printed in the United States of America
First Edition, November 2020

A Jesus Mission Publishing
PO Box 872601 Vancouver, Washington 98687
Ordering Information:
www.ourmissioninchrist.com
www.andyziesemer.com
www.ajmpublishing.org

For orders by U.S. trade bookstores and wholesalers, contact AJM Publishing:
accounts@ajmpublishing.org or visit www.ajmpublishing.org

CONTENTS

FOREWORD 14
INTRODUCTION 16
I. UNDERSTANDING THE MISSION OF CHRIST 20
    WHY DID JESUS REALLY COME 22
    WHAT WAS HIS MISSION 26
    HIS MISSION MUST BECOME OURS 32
    THE COMMISSION 36
    THE VOICE BY WHICH WE ARE SENT 38
    THE COMMAND ITSELF 44
    THE INCLUDED TASKS 48
        BAPTIZE THEM 64

TEACH THEM	67
BEAR WITNESS	70
PREACH THE REMISSION OF SINS	71
PAULS INSTRUCTIONS	77
WAIT	79

THE PROMISE OF THE HOLY SPIRIT ... 82

HE WILL BE WITH US	86
DON'T GET DISTRACTED	88
THERE WILL BE SIGNS	89
THEIR DIVERSITY	91
THEIR PURPOSE	93
SIGNS AND FRUIT	94

JESUS EXPLAINS GIFTS ... 96

PAUL EXPLAINS GIFTS	97
THE WHEN AND THE WHERE	100
THE GREATEST GIFT: LOVE	102
THE CHURCH WILL GROW	104
TRANSFORMED PEOPLE	
CHANGE THE WAY THEY LIVE	106
WHAT'S THE PROOF?	109

II. PREPARING TO LIVE ON MISSION ... 114

AM I A MISSIONARY? ... 116

GENERAL CALLINGS	118
SPECIFIC CALLINGS	119
BIBLICAL EXAMPLES OF SPECIFIC CALLINGS	120
AM I CALLED TO GO OR TO STAY?	124

DEVELOPING A HEART LIKE JESUS ... 126
IMITATING JESUS ... 130
FORGIVING LIKE JESUS DID ... 132
SHIFTING OUR FOCUS ... 136
FOCUS ON ETERNAL THINGS ... 137
PUT OFF THESE THINGS ... 139
PUT ON THESE THINGS ... 140
THE SPIRIT EQUIPS US ... 142
HE CONVICTS US ... 143
RECOGNIZING THE VOICE OF THE HOLY SPIRIT ... 145
THE NECESSITY OF BEING SPIRITUALLY MATURE ... 148
WHERE DO WE LOOK? ... 150
HOW DO WE ACT? ... 152
WHAT DO WE SAY? ... 156
TAKE IT SLOW ... 158
THE ROLE OF A HEALTHY CHURCH COMMUNITY ... 162
PRAYER ... 166
FASTING ... 172
JESUS FASTED ... 175
HIS DISCIPLES FASTED ... 177

III. BECOMING PEOPLE WHO WILL CHANGE THE WORLD ... 180
LIVING ON PURPOSE ... 182
ENGAGING ON PURPOSE EVERY DAY ... 183
BUT I'M INTROVERTED ... 184
STOP SIGNS ... 186

- CULTURAL INFLUENCES 188
- LIVING OBEDIENTLY 191

RESPONDING TO CHAOS AND DEATH 194
- CHAOS 195
- DEATH 196

AVOIDING THE APPEARANCE OF EVIL 198
- PERMISSABLE VS BENEFICIAL 200

PUT ON THE ARMOR 202
- THE BELT OF TRUTH 204
- THE ARMOR OF RIGHTEOUSNESS 204
- FOR SHOES, PUT ON PEACE 206
- THE SHIELD OF FAITH 207
- THE HELMET OF SALVATION 208
- THE SWORD OF THE SPIRIT 210
- PRAY IN THE SPIRIT 211

YOU CAN'T CONTROL WHAT OTHERS SAY 214

THE IMPORTANCE OF REALLY GOOD RELATIONSHIPS 218
- BECOMING RECONCILERS 219
- THE LOVE OF CHRIST COMPELS US 221

THE IMPORTANCE OF BEING A PART OF THE CHURCH 226
- WHAT IS THE RIGHT KIND OF CHURCH? 231
- BUILD RELATIONSHIPS THAT CAUSE YOU TO GROW 233
- LEARNING ON PURPOSE 234

STAYING HEALTHY 238

Our Mission In Christ

DOING THE WORD..	242
GOING INTO THE WORLD..	244
DON'T MISS THE POINT...	246
DOING WHAT YOU LOVE..	248
BECOMING PEOPLE	
WHO WILL CHANGE THE WORLD...	250

Contents

OUR MISSION IN CHRIST

FOREWORD

The subtitle of this book sums up Andy Ziesemer: *Becoming People Who Will Change The World*. That is who he is. For the last decade I have been inspired by Andy's vision for missions. We have spent countless hours on two continents talking about the Lord and how to reach more people with the Gospel, and there is always coffee involved!

    Andy is not afraid to dream, to pray and to take risks. I remember sitting in a restaurant in Budapest listening to him talk about the dream of sending people around the world doing music and barista ministry. Who thinks like that? Andy!

Forword

And the result has been young people around the world doing what they love whilst sharing about Who they love.

I am grateful for Andy's friendship. He makes you feel like you could be a part of how he sees the world (and you can!). God wants to reach the world with His extravagant love and He is using ordinary people to do so. How beautiful is that?

If you are reading this, keep on reading because Andy's heart and passion for Jesus and His mission are all over these pages!

Phil Metzger
Missionary in Eastern Europe for 20+ years
Pastor at Calvary Chapel San Diego

INTRO

I was sitting in the oversized chairs at a local coffee shop ignoring the activity around me, focused entirely on the book in my hand. A man in his late seventies sat down directly across from me, and uncomfortably close to me. He stared at me quietly, until finally, upon realizing he was not going to release his gaze until I had engaged him, I said, "Hello."

He replied kindly with a greeting, and immediately began to speak.

He wasted no time getting right to the point of sitting across from me. He wanted to tell me about Jesus. He began to expound into a well-intended (although slightly confusing) sharing of the Gospel with me. Somehow he got into talking about Noah's ark, and rambled along with a few other stories, but his ultimate point was direct and clear: he wanted me to know who Jesus was.

I didn't stop him from speaking, rather, I marveled at what was happening. I live in the suburbs of a large U.S. city. I encounter many, many persons in my daily life.

At the time I was 28 years old, and that was the first time in my life a stranger had shared the Gospel with me.

I remember this so precisely because I journaled this event, having been a moment of note to me. It had taken nearly three decades for someone to approach me, assume I had not heard the name of Jesus, and take the time to share it.

I grew up in church, having had both a biological and church family that taught me the truth of the Gospel. But outside of that context, nobody had ever bore witness of what Jesus had done for me.

I've spent the better portion of my life serving either in a local church or on the mission field. I've shared the Gospel with thousands upon thousands of people. I have lived a large part of my life taking for granted the truth of the Gospel that was taught to me as a child. I realized that even though I am living in a huge city filled with believers, most of the people in any public space I enter during my day have probably not heard who Jesus is and why that matters.

I know that I am a broken, wretched man, wrought with sin and failure. But I am also a son of the living God, bought with a price, and covered by the grace of God. For this reason, I must share the hope that I have.

As a believer transformed by the restorative work of Jesus, it becomes vital that as my life is transformed by an understanding of the Word of God, I learn to do the mission of Christ in my daily life.

The imperative of sharing the Gospel with those who don't yet believe lay not solely in the hands of clergy and vocational missionaries. If you have this understanding and knowledge, it falls also to you. Having a transformed life demands that you live differently. The goal of this book is to understand the mission of Jesus with more clarity, to prepare our hearts and align our actions to reflect a transformed life, and begin actively pursuing those who are lost.

We must begin to live out the mission of Christ together as the Church. Gaining a right understanding of the mission of Jesus means that we are going to begin actively living on a Jesus mission.

This book is an invitation to all, to pick up a sword and join the fight. This is an invitation to submit your life to the Word of God. This is an invitation to walk with the boldness to live on mission every day; be it a foreign field, in your neighborhood, or in your home.

Introduction

PART ONE.

UNDERSTANDING THE MISSION OF CHRIST

WHY DID JESUS REALLY COME?

The Gospels tell us the story of Jesus and give us clear understanding of God's desire for our redemption through Jesus' life, death on the cross, and resurrection. Through His life we see the expressed love of God manifested in His personhood. From His interactions with the people He lived among, to the prayers He prayed for us, we see the love of God enacted for us through the mission of Christ on the earth.

Jesus came to restore the brokenness caused by sin and unite us back to God. In the coming pages it is my hope that you will come to understand more of the reason Jesus came.

To both begin and continue this process of understanding, we need only look to the Word of God. One of my favorite places in the Word where Jesus reveals His heart for the lost is in Luke 19. I want to point out two specific things in this section as we begin.

First, **Jesus looked at people.** Our prime example is when we read that He was on route to another town and He came to the place where Zacchaeus was sitting in a tree. We see Him come to the place, pause, and look up (Luke 19:5).

I love that short phrase, "*He looked up.*" This sentence shows us that God's eyes are constantly looking towards the lost. He knew exactly where this man of small stature would be sitting, waiting, and watching. He then turned His eyes intentionally toward him. Jesus said: "*Zacchaeus, hurry and come down, for I must stay at your house today*" (Luke 19:5). His short, powerful statement changed Zacchaeus' life forever.

It should also change ours.

For us to accurately understand Jesus' mission on earth, we need to realize that He stopped for people. He looked at them. He acknowledged them where they were, in their brokenness, shame, failures, and weakness.

Imagine Zacchaeus' surprise when in the throngs of people, Jesus stopped and made eye contact specifically with him. As I have traveled the world I have often found that the most impactful moments we have with people are the ones in which we stop, look someone in the eye, and engage with them. Regardless of which nation they are a citizen of, what people group they are in, or what past they have, people matter to Jesus. If they matter to Him, they must also matter to us.

Second, we see that **Jesus urged Zacchaeus toward Himself.** He is still urging us toward Himself today. Personally I am so glad He is constantly drawing us toward Himself through the working of the Spirit in our lives. In the life of the believer, we know that the Holy Spirit is drawing us towards God through conviction and by transforming our desires.

With lost people, He is always urging them to come into relationship with Him. Sometimes people just need to be made aware of this reality, being presented the truth of God through the preaching of the Gospel.

We are commanded to engage in the Gospel as the Gospel changes us.

In verse six we see Zacchaeus hurry down from the tree and receive Jesus joyfully. Through our personal experience and the Word of God, we know this is not always going to be the response we see when we offer people the truth. Often the truth will be rejected, as we see occur in Acts 19. But that rejection doesn't change the imperative we've been given: we must be willing to give a reason for the hope that we have (1 Peter 3).

As soon as Zacchaeus encountered Jesus, he became repentant of his shortcomings and failures.

A true encounter with Jesus will draw us to repentance.

A true encounter causes the lost—even those who don't

Part One: Understanding

yet recognize their lostness—to realize that they have been found! The result is a changed life.

Recognizing Jesus' heart for the lost is critical for us to understand, especially if we are people who desire to be missional. Jesus says in Luke 19:10 "...the Son of Man has come to seek and to save the lost."

WHAT WAS HIS MISSION?

The answer is simple: Jesus' mission on earth is to do the work of God, unifying all of humanity with their Creator.

Our ever-developing understanding of the mission of Christ is directly correlated to the health of our relationship with Him. **The greater the depth of intimacy we have with Him, the greater the depth of understanding of His heart for people is revealed to us.** As we understand His grace more and more, our hearts are being transformed into the same as that of Christ. The immeasurability of His grace was revealed in that He—to do the will of His father—willingly surrendered His Godship to hold with us, the broken humble state of humanity. This heart is revealed to us through the Word of God

Itself. In John 17:20-21, we see His prayer for the believers reveal the deepest longings of His own heart:

> *I pray not only for these, but also for those who believe in me through their word. May they all be one, as you, Father, are in me and I am in you. May they also be in us, so that the world may believe you sent me.*

Jesus came to restore brokenness in relationships. By God's sovereign design and for the purposes of His own glory, this is accomplished through a relationship with Him. God's longing for a deep relationship with us was revealed in the act of creating man, and then again at the creation of woman, where it shows us that God knew Adam needed another relationship to exist.

It is amazing to consider that with the creation of each and every single new person on earth, the opportunity for a loving relationship is birthed alongside them. Yet, so many never fully understand the joy that comes from having this type of relationship. My hope is that in reading this book we are pushed to invite others into those deep relationships, both with Christ and with each other, as we go to be the Church in the world.

The absolute desire of God is that not a single one of us should perish. We know this by reading His own thoughts about us, revealed to us in John 3:16-17. But sadly many will perish without Him. In fact, many are actively perishing today, living lives separate from the fullness of joy and the confidence of an eternal hope that is promised by Him.

In John 6:38-40, we see Jesus open His mouth and speak God's heart on the matter:

> *For I have come down from heaven, not to do my own will, but the will of him who sent me. This is the will of him who sent me: that I should lose none of those he has given me but should raise them up on the last day. For this is the will of my Father: that everyone who sees the Son and believes in him will have eternal life, and I will raise him up on the last day.*

The will of God is that every single person in the history of the world might have the eternity with God that He designed for us. When Jesus says, "I should lose none of those he has given me," He is telling us that He was sent to save us all! We are that which He is speaking of!

"*Should we believe...*" that is the key. Every person should see the Son and believe in Him. And so, the mission of Christ for us begins to come into focus. We point others to believe, repent, and receive that new hope.

But sharing that is hard.

As I have traveled the road, many ask my perspectives on the great darkness that surrounds people today. The overwhelming thought is that darkness and sin are so heavily impacting our world; sharing the truth in the midst of darkness must be of extreme difficulty. There is a general fear for those who are so lost that they will likely never be found. Yet our call remains.

I can declare with surety to you today, that when we understand the person of Christ for who He is—and also the mission of Christ for what it is—our eyes are opened. When Jesus says, "I am the light of the world" in John 8:12, He is speaking not only about the truth of His character, but about the nature of what He does as we live on mission! He brings the light into the darkness as we go.

We who walk in the light can be sure that we do not walk in darkness, even when it feels as though the light is out. When we go into dark places, light must always prevail. The illumination at work within communities and dark nations is a steadily shining beacon declaring that He is in fact actively changing lives today.

The work of Christ was final, yet the mission we undertake together today is temporal. At some point in our human future, the command to share the Gospel will reach its end because Christ will indeed return for His Church. Until that moment comes, we must live on a Jesus mission: making known the simplicity of His love for those who are dying.

We are called to be the very people who will change the state of the world.

John Piper hits the nail on the head when he says, "*Mission exists because worship doesn't*" (*Let The Nations Be Glad*). Since the creation of man, the point of everything has been the glorification of God through relationship with God. Even now, the brokenness that accompanied the fall of man is actively being restored through the cross. Jesus came to become the final sacrifice needed for us to have a reconciled relationship with God. We need to be people on mission, until all of creation is declaring the praise of God, either on earth or in heaven.

What was Jesus' mission on earth?

To do God's will on earth (John 6:38).

To be light in a dark world (John 8:12).

To become the final sacrifice needed for us to have reconciled relationship with God (2 Corinthians 5:21).

Part One: Understanding

HIS MISSION MUST BECOME OURS

The greatest understanding of the mission of Christ comes when we understand our own miserable failures as a separating factor in our relationship with God. As we discover the depths of His grace in our own lives, it begins to prepare us to engage in the work. I am a sinner, but I have been saved by the work of the cross. **Our inward transformation will result in outward declaration.**

I have seen far too many people accept the free gift of salvation without engaging in a full and proper response. We will examine a few of these responses in the coming pages, but if we are to understand His mission to the depth at which we take it as our own, I believe we have to start in the Word.

How do we do this? What is considered a full and proper response? How do we effectively become a part of those who are doing the work we are called to?

As our lives become transformed by the truth of the Bible and the actions we take become ones taken through the lens of the Gospel, we are surely becoming more spiritually mature. **Growth in spiritual maturity results in an inevitable advance of the Gospel,** the advance of which is a work entrusted to us by God. We have been shown how to do it, and instructed by Jesus to engage. To fully make His mission our own and begin changing the world, we must start in the Word.

It would be good to clarify here that it is **not** by our works that we are saved. Scripture makes this clear, it is by Jesus' work on the cross that we have our salvation. The works we do become a response to His work, not an effort of our own to accomplish anything. Scripture gives us very clear commands in terms of our proper response to Jesus. I believe the Word will speak sufficiently for itself. None of us escape the need for Jesus. "*For everyone has sinned; we all fall short of God's glorious standard*" (Romans 3:23).

Jesus came because of the unfathomable love of God for His creation. We fall desperately short of God's glory and so the perfect person of Jesus came to earth to become sin for us, to take the punishment for all mankind. As God's own Son,

He took every bit of God's wrath so that we might have access directly to God through Jesus. He came to give us life where we had only death.

The greater our understanding of our own need for Him, the greater our understanding of others' needs for Him becomes clear.

Jesus came to save the world and give us life through Him. Our deepest longings will be solely satisfied in Him. *"Jesus replied, "I am the bread of life. Whoever comes to me will never be hungry again. Whoever believes in me will never be thirsty"* (John 6:35).

To know Jesus and have relationship with God is incredibly simple. You must believe that He was and is the risen Son of God. Then upon the confession of your sins and your need for Him, the Bible says you are saved (Romans 10:9-13).

He is actively fulfilling His mission on earth, bringing us into restored relationship with God. That is His mission, so what is ours?

Part One: Understanding

THE COMMISSION

It has been stated by many that we have been given the Great Commission, not the great suggestion. These texts of commission are no less important of a command for the followers of Jesus than that of loving our neighbor. Any command by Jesus should be found equally important in our lives. Hence there is a vital need for the believer to be constantly in the Word of God, letting Jesus' words and teachings penetrate every part of our soul.

In reality, obeying the part about loving your neighbors (Leviticus 19:18, Matthew 19:19, Mark 12:33) would in itself mandate that you share the hope you have with them!

True love for another person gives you an immense desire

to see them come into the same joyful relationship with the Creator that you also are in.

So how do we personalize this command? **How do we actually make His mission ours?** How does taking this action result in a changed world?

To begin to realize the answers to these questions, we will look at the actual commands of Jesus. I will address this in four segments:

- The voice by which we are sent.
- The command itself.
- The included tasks.
- The promise of the Holy Spirit.

THE VOICE BY WHICH WE ARE SENT

From the start of humanity, the fragile, created human has been the plan of God to bring the rightful Glory of God to Himself for the rest of eternity. The whole of scripture points us to Jesus. Jesus restores us to God. God rejoices in and is glorified by our restored unity with Him.

The very voice by which we are sent to humanity is the voice of the One who created humanity.

Our sending power is fully authoritative.

It is the very voice that cast the stars in the sky. It is the same voice by which the mountains were formed and the seas were stilled. The voice of Jesus **is** the very voice of God.

Part One: Understanding

> *In the beginning was the Word, and the Word was with God, and the Word was God. He was with God in the beginning. All things were created through him, and apart from him not one thing was created that has been created. In him was life, and that life was the light of men. That light shines in the darkness, and yet the darkness did not overcome it.*
> John 1:1-4

By this account, when we hear the voice of Jesus telling us to live on mission, we are listening to directives from the very Creator of our souls. We oughtn't take these words lightly. We must respond. These words demand action.

Understanding the Truth

To set the stage and build the foundation of His authority, Jesus used what He knew His followers would understand. The historical scriptures that they would have learned prophesied of His coming:

He told them,

> *These are my words that I spoke to you while I was still with you—that everything written about me in the Law of Moses, the Prophets, and the Psalms must be fulfilled." Then he opened their minds to understand the Scriptures. He also said to them, "This is what is*

> *written: The Messiah will suffer and rise from the dead the third day.*
> *Luke 24:44-46*

Jesus uses their understanding of the scriptures, as He had opened their minds to so understand. This is in itself a role of the Spirit of God. *"When the Spirit of truth comes, he will guide you into all the truth"* (John 16:13). It was the Spirit's own job to reveal to them Jesus' authority.

They would have known these scriptures and believed them to be true. So, as Jesus often does, He used their finite understanding and knowledge to point to Himself.

Authority from Whom?

All authority by which we act as we live on mission comes from God Himself. When the voice of God bears witness to His own credibility, we—if a person who believes Him to be who He says He is—have no reason to doubt what He says.

Jesus makes it clear that He is sent by the Father in John chapter five, where He lays out the authority of His own witness.

> *The Father who sent me has himself testified about me. You have not heard his voice at any time, and you haven't seen his form. You don't have his word residing in you, because you don't believe the one he sent. You pore*

Part One: Understanding

> *over the Scriptures because you think you have eternal life in them, and yet they testify about me. But you are not willing to come to me so that you may have life.*
> John 5:37-40

In His address of those to whom He first gave the Great Commission, Jesus began with His authority. When we go now, we go as ambassadors bearing His name, operating under the authority of the very Creator God Himself. We have no reason to go timidly, but rather ought to be standing boldly on His name. An ambassador speaks clearly and boldly for the one who sends him.

Jesus came near and said to them, "*All authority has been given to me in heaven and on earth*" (Matthew 28:18).

Then He said to them, "*Go into all the world and preach the gospel to all creation*" (Mark 16:15).

Jesus said to them again, "*Peace be with you. As the Father has sent me, I also send you*" (John 20:21).

We need not question our sent-ness. It is clearly attested to by the unity of the Gospel writers.

We are sent, so we must go.

Jesus' Prayer

I am so encouraged to know that Jesus, in His own prayers, spoke to God on our behalf. He prayed for us to have the same level of unity that He Himself had with the Father! Think this through: the very words of Jesus were:

> *I pray not only for these, but also for those who believe in me through their word. May they all be one, as you, Father, are in me and I am in you. May they also be in us, so that the world may believe you sent me. I have given them the glory you have given me, so that they may be one as we are one.*
> John 17:20-22

He has sent us, yes. But He desires that we be in such close relationship with God that we might have the same level of intimacy that Jesus Himself has with the Father! Oh, the longing of my own heart, that I might have this.

Imagine the level of boldness we would employ in our daily lives if we were so assured of this proximity with God. If Jesus is praying that we might be so close as to know the very thoughts of God, we can know that it is indeed possible!

This possibility comes when we deeply understand and begin to live a life embracing the role of the Holy Spirit within us.

Part One: Understanding

THE COMMAND ITSELF

In now knowing and being assured of the authority of the command, we must examine the command itself.

This directive is not something we need to search for long, because it is a one word answer. Go!

"*Go therefore*" (Matthew 28:19).
"*Go into all the world*" (Mark 16:15).
"*As the Father has sent me, I also send you*" (John 20:21).

These are simply the words of Jesus.

The command itself is living and active, because **His** voice is living and active. The command itself never dies as it will continue unchanged until Christ's return, both for us individually and for the rest of humanity as we know it. Our job is simply to obey.

So why do we go? Why do we open our mouths to tell others? I like how John Piper says it: "*What do we do with news? We tell it!*"

We speak news because it is worth speaking. Entire global industries have been built around the sole task of telling the world what is happening. If we have such vital, transformative news as we do, we ought to be in the business of telling it!

In Christian circles, you have likely heard the common phrase: "Preach the Gospel always, and if necessary, use words." I propose to you that this statement in fact contradicts the very words of Jesus! **To claim that you can preach the Gospel without opening your mouth is to not fully understand the Gospel.**

God's plan for the redemption of the world is that broken people, redeemed by Jesus, will declare this redemption to those around them. Active Gospel declaration requires you to speak.

Some point to this text when making excuses for keeping their mouths closed: "They will know we are Christians by our love." Yes. Love is the attestation of a changed life. However, Paul makes it very clear in Romans 10 that no one will call on Him of whom they have not believed. Nobody will believe anything about someone of whom they have never heard. And nobody hears without somebody speaking. And we clearly know that nobody preaches unless they are sent; meaning, some authoritative power must in fact be doing the sending. When Paul works this thought backwards, we see that if anyone is going to believe, they indeed must hear.

You are charged with the task of opening your mouth. I submit to you that to "*Go into all the world*" requires action and intentionality (Mark 16:15).

The tasks we will examine next are a part of the Great Commission. We must undertake them together if we are to be obedient and see Gospel-invoked change occur in our temporary world.

Part One: Understanding

THE INCLUDED TASKS

Our first task is belief. It is in this that we are saved. All these other tasks follow the transformation of our heart from unbelief to belief. The disciples were eager to do tasks and call them "the works of God," but Jesus simplified it: believe.

> What can we do to perform the works of God?" they asked. Jesus replied: "This is the work of God—that you believe in the one he has sent.
> John 6:28-29

Part One: Understanding

Romans 10:9 says,

> *If you confess with your mouth, "Jesus is Lord," and believe in your heart that God raised him from the dead, you will be saved.*

Our belief is in itself a transforming thing. No other piece of living on mission occurs until this has occurred.

Many people aim to do good works, hoping that it will accomplish for them the restitution of their souls. This simply does not work. No work we can undertake will restore our relationship with God. Solely Jesus has that power.

Many believers I've met have spent their lives doing good things while missing out on the whole point: relationship with Jesus glorifies God by bringing us back to Him. We see this exemplified when people came to Jesus saying they have been doing works in His name, casting out demons, healing people, etc. He says, "I never knew you."

Oh, how sad those words would be to hear. To live your life, wasting your efforts and time on a pointless attempt at perfection. We are only made perfect in Jesus.

All of these things which Jesus commands of us in the Great Commission only occur after belief; after we've entered into a healthy, restored, and God-glorifying relationship with Himself.

We will now expand on what the Great Commission lists as our next steps, but stop here for a moment with me.

If you are not in a right relationship with God, I plead with you to confess your need of God right now. Accept the gift of grace that has been given, and allow Jesus to transform your heart.

To begin our journey towards a better understanding of the mission, we will explore these specific topics at greater depth:

- Making disciples.
- Baptizing disciples.
- Teaching them to observe the commandments.
- Bearing witness.
- Preaching the remission of sins.
- Waiting for the power to go.

Make Disciples

"We should never be shocked by the spiritual immaturity of believers, but we should also never be content with it."
—Richard Camino

Matthew 28:19-20 is probably one of the most quoted, discussed, and famous Great Commission verses. This is for good reason, as it is explicitly clear on our next steps.

After Jesus commands us to go, the first task He gives us is that of making disciples of all the nations.

Discipleship is one of the most commonly spoken words

Part One: Understanding

in organized church, yet I fear it is frequently the command that we are least intentional with. If we are truly going to be obedient to the Biblical commands and see our Christian communities grow in healthy ways, then we need to become more diligent in this very specific area.

Without truly intentional engagement, we will too easily drop the ball on this one. It makes sense though, because it comes at an incredibly high cost for us personally.

Literally hundreds of books have been published on this topic through the development of Christendom, bearing detailed, longwinded instruction on how to curate the perfect disciple. Yet still so many believers are lacking the true spiritual depth that comes from this process. Why is that? How can hundreds of books describe the process for us in such detail, yet so many believers remain in infancy?

Perhaps we're overcomplicating it.

The commandment to make disciples will cost you your time, your energy, and probably even your money. No person is discipled without the heavy investment of time and deep relationship. **What's hardest for me is realizing that we are to pay this cost even when those we invest in seem not to care or are even ungrateful.**

Jesus set the pace and example for this throughout His short life on earth.

Jesus spoke aloud to thousands, yet lived alongside only a few every day. Over His lifetime He ministered to countless numbers of people as He traveled from city to city. However, those He traveled with had a much closer perspective on who He was and how He lived His life. Those are the types of disciples we should be making. The kind we are learning to follow Jesus with every single day.

In his book, *The Lost Art of Disciple Making*, LeRoy Eims speaks to the amount of time true discipleship will require of you:

> *Likeminded, trustworthy, competent men are not made on a production line like automobiles in an assembly plant. They are carefully and prayerfully developed under the loving guidance of a wise trainer who spends much time on his knees praying for them. In an age of nearly instant everything, we must discipline ourselves to think in terms of quality.*

When we know of a person who has decided to follow Christ, we cannot just hope that a local church pastor will scoop them into their arms, invite them into their home, and begin engaging in discipleship.

Let me challenge you: **if you are a part of that person's life and have the capacity and understanding with which to begin the process, then it is officially your commission to invite them over.**

Spiritually maturing persons continually point each other towards Jesus. That is how disciples are made.

Modern Discipleship

There is neither an antiquated version nor a relevant model of discipleship. There is just simply discipleship. While the tools that we have available to communicate and work together change weekly, being an effective disciple-maker is not accomplished in the way you use technology. Rather, the test is in their ability to teach those around them that the Word is sufficient for all situations.

Disciples are made the same way today as they were made during the life of Jesus: in close proximity and in deep relationship.

It is in the depth of relationship that we encounter conflict. It is in the tasks we undertake together that we are given the chance to show what it means to follow Jesus, rather than just talking about how to do it. It is in the moments of grief we share together that we affirm our eternal perspective and hope in Jesus Christ.

A person living out the mission of Christ will do as Christ did: bring a few people close, live out their life alongside them, bear with them in love and patience, and teach them all that Jesus commanded us.

Then, as seasons change in their life and people come and go, they will begin the process all over again. A person who is changing the world through effective discipleship will repeat this process in new contexts. They will not fear when the person chooses to leave or moves to another town.

Until the day you die, you are to be engaged in the work of discipleship.

Jesus' Method of Discipleship

"To have people become involved with you, you must first become involved with them."

- LeRoy Eims

When we dissect the Gospel accounts of Jesus' life, we begin to see the approach and method He used to create healthy disciples. He called them, taught them, involved them, pointed them to God, set them apart, and sent them.

I love the prayer that Jesus prays for His disciples in John 17. For the purpose of this next section, I think we should start there. If we examine His prayer for the disciples, we can see both what He told God He accomplished and what He ultimately desired for them.

> *I have revealed your name to the people you gave me from the world. They were yours, you gave them to me, and they have kept your word. Now they know that everything you have given me is from you, because I have given them the words you gave me. They have received them and have known for certain that I came from you.*

Part One: Understanding

> *They have believed that you sent me. "I pray for them. I am not praying for the world but for those you have given me, because they are yours. Everything I have is yours, and everything you have is mine, and I am glorified in them. I am no longer in the world, but they are in the world, and I am coming to you. Holy Father, protect them by your name that you have given me, so that they may be one as we are one. While I was with them, I was protecting them by your name that you have given me. I guarded them and not one of them is lost, except the son of destruction, so that the Scripture may be fulfilled. Now I am coming to you, and I speak these things in the world so that they may have my joy completed in them. I have given them your word. The world hated them because they are not of the world, just as I am not of the world. I am not praying that you take them out of the world but that you protect them from the evil one. They are not of the world, just as I am not of the world. Sanctify them by the truth; your word is truth. As you sent me into the world, I also have sent them into the world. I sanctify myself for them, so that they also may be sanctified by the truth.*
> John 17:6-19

This is not a book focused entirely on the methods of discipleship, as that focus in itself could consume the entirety of these pages. Yet, I believe for us to adequately examine the Great Commission, it demands we give it our attention.

I want to observe five elements in Jesus' prayer, and examine His heart for His disciples as we learn to create them. If we can pattern our heart for those we teach the Gospel to, to match that of Jesus, I believe we will be plotting a course for healthy discipleship.

- He taught them the right perspective of God.
- He taught them the right perspective of His words.
- He taught them the route to the Father.
- He set them apart.
- He sent them out.

He Taught Them the Right Perspective of God

> "Now they know that everything you have given me is from you."
>
> John 17:7

In Jesus' prayer, we see Him telling the Father that the disciples' perspectives had been aligned to have a correct understanding of God. He has established in their lives an understanding that all He is and has done up to that point is an expression of the very heart of God. By coming as a human man, He showed them that God's heart is indeed for humanity.

Part One: Understanding

He manifested the person of God, revealing the character of God.

In John 14:7 He tells them, "*If you had known me, you would have known my Father also; and from now on you know him and have seen him.*" He is putting into right perspective their understanding of His person!

Right away, in the next verse Philip says, "*Show us the Father, and that's enough for us*" (John 14:8).

Jesus rebukes him, but also teaches him in this moment: "*Have I been among you all this time and you do not know me, Philip? The one who has seen me has seen the Father. How can you say, 'Show us the Father'?*" (John 14:9).

He teaches them again that any words which come from His mouth are ones that He speaks with the same authority as the Father. He goes so far as to say, "*Believe me that I am in the Father and the Father is in me. Otherwise, believe because of the works themselves*" (John 14:10-11).

The works He was doing validated His claim. He taught the disciples to understand that He was in fact God. He is the Word Himself, and He lived that out in front of them, teaching them this truth.

As a disciple-maker, our role is teaching people to have a larger understanding of who God is.

With verse seven of this prayer, Jesus tells God that He has given the disciples a depth of understanding they did not have prior to knowing Him. They now understand that all things come from God. The miracles that Jesus performed were acts performed by the sovereign God. The words that Jesus spoke were the very words of God. Jesus came as God, and the disciples believed this to be true.

He Taught Them the Right Perspective of His Words

"I have given them the words you gave me. They have received them and have known for certain that I came from you. They have believed that you sent me."

John 17:8

When the disciples came into understanding that Jesus was God, the words of Jesus as He spoke to them were being spoken in the voice of God. Imagine being them in the moment when they came into the understanding that if the Father was speaking through Jesus, they were hearing the voice of God every day as they lived alongside Him.

    I imagine there were moments in following Jesus that would have been immensely overwhelming. We read of other moments, though, when those walking with Him sound like blundering fools. They were arguing over who was going to be greater. They were forgetting that Jesus had fed five thousand men when faced with feeding four thousand only a week later. **The disciples were constantly afraid that there was no solution to their needs, while standing next to the One who meets every need.**

The disciples lacked much understanding, but still Jesus imparted to them the truth of His own words as the very words of God, and they received them (John 14:14).

If we are making disciples as Jesus did, we will be teaching people the authority of the Word of God, and giving right perspective to both the origin of the Word and its power.

Jesus gave His disciples the Word.

He Taught Them the Route to the Father

"I pray for them. I am not praying for the world but for those you have given me, because they are yours. Everything I have is yours, and everything you have is mine, and I am glorified in them. I am no longer in the world, but they are in the world, and I am coming to you. Holy Father, protect them by your name that you have given me, so that they may be one as we are one."

John 17:9-11

Jesus prays for those He loves. Here He is praying specifically for His disciples after teaching them that the only way to have a relationship with God is through the Son. He, Himself, **is** the route to God. Those He taught understood this.

By being in relationship with Jesus, God was being glorified in their lives. Jesus prays that the disciples would be kept through the name of the Father, that they might be one in the same way that God and Jesus are one. So what are we to draw from this piece of His prayer?

Jesus has taught His followers that the only route to God was Himself. He had established with them that nobody comes to the Father but by the Son (John 6:44). He is praying that God would keep them in that knowledge, that God would hold close those who come to the Father through the Son.

People making disciples should be teaching, that in all things, the only means of salvation is Jesus. We cannot accomplish salvation with our works, nor our most excellent undertakings. There is only one way. It's just Jesus.

He Set Them Apart

"While I was with them, I was protecting them by your name that you have given me. I guarded them and not one of them is lost, except the son of destruction, so that the Scripture may be fulfilled. Now I am coming to you, and I speak these things in the world so that they may have my joy completed in them. I have given them your word. The world hated them because they are not of the world, just as I am not of the world. I am not praying that you take

> *them out of the world but that you protect them from the evil one. They are not of the world, just as I am not of the world. Sanctify them by the truth; your word is truth."*
>
> John 17:12-17

Sanctified. What an absolutely powerful word this is.

We have been set apart. We have been set into the purposes of God as He works in and through us for His own eternal glory. We have been redeemed despite our many failures, and we have been chosen by God.

This part of the prayer we see in John 17 should truly excite believers! Jesus is saying that He is keeping us secure. He is praying that we might have the same inexplicable joy as He had. He is praying that we would be assured in having His Word, and saying that God is keeping us from the evil one!

We who follow Jesus are not of this world, just as Jesus was not of this world. We are guaranteed an eternity with God. How great is this! How great is our God! And how great should our response be to this knowledge!

As we disciple people, we should be pointing them to this truth: they have been set apart for the glory of God, resulting in our doing good works **for** God, because we are loved. We should assure the believer who is growing in spiritual maturity that they are a child of the living God. Oh, what blessed assurance.

Jesus' prayer should excite the believer. His prayer should

drive us to respond by earnestly sharing the hope that we have in eternity with those we encounter. This hope will ultimately lead us and those around us to respond in the Great Commission. Being sent is the final part of this prayer for the disciple, which we will address in the next section.

I would like to observe one last thing from this text: in His prayer, Jesus actually prays **for us**, that we would **not** be taken out of this world.

Think on this for a moment. It is the will of God, the very prayer of Jesus that we would be here, in this very form, for as long a time as God allows.

I've heard too many of my Christian brothers and sisters speak longingly for Jesus to return and their time on earth to end. I do understand this. I recently lost my father to cancer, who in his final days was eager to see Jesus and be done with the misery of his frail human body.

It is appointed for man to die, and this will happen in God's timing. But consider this prayer for the disciples by Jesus: that God would **not** take us from this earth, but that we should be kept from the evil one.

The completion of our human existence which occurs at death is truly precious in the sight of God. We read that *"The death of his faithful ones is valuable in the Lord's sight"* (Psalm 116:15). But, **until that time when God has appointed for you to die, you are to be living on mission!**

My good friend, Brian Grant, regularly says that he wants

to go into heaven with the afterburners on. I love that picture of us diving into the finish line. We who understand the Gospel fully should have a renewed energy for the work to which we are called, to the end of our days.

I pray that Jesus' prayer would resonate with you today. That you, though you long for heaven, would stay focused and engaged in the mission of Christ.

Jesus desired that His disciples live in the very world He declared hated us, just a few verses before. Why would He want us here?! Especially if the world hates us?

It is because we truly do have a reason to be here! The unification of God and man occurs in the lives of those who have heard the Gospel! And so we must preach it.

He Sent Them Out

"As you sent me into the world, I also have sent them into the world. I sanctify myself for them, so that they also may be sanctified by the truth."

John 17:18-19

Jesus was sent and now He is sending us. Jesus was the first to come on mission, so He knows a thing or two about being a sent human. He gave up His heavenly, Godhead comforts to come live as a man in brokenness. In pain, He bore the full weight of our sins on Himself in agony on the cross. **He fully understands that which He is sending us to do.**

We are daily being sanctified by the truth of the Word, which is Jesus Himself, so that we can be in perfect relationship with God once more.

BAPTIZE THEM

Another action for us to undertake as we learn to obey the Word of God is the act of baptizing those walking in repentance. It is a vital part of the Christian life.

Do not misunderstand this concept. Baptism is not a saving act in itself. No person is redeemed in the eyes of God by being either sprinkled or fully submerged in water.

This is, however, something we are told to do. Having an adequate grasp of its purpose and role in the believer's life is important. Then, as people living on mission, we are to go and do it! Jesus tells us to baptize those who believe in the name of the Father, the Son, and the Holy Spirit.

Throughout the New Testament, when new believers entered into relationship with God, baptism was the next step.

Sadly, today we have reversed that order in many of our religious circles and denominations. In some circles we baptize children before they have even made a decision to follow

Christ. This literally defeats the entire purpose. **We baptize believers to make an outward expression of our internal transformation.**

When we submerge a person, it is a marvelous picture of the burial of the old life. Then as they reemerge, it represents the new living person; being raised as Christ was raised from the dead and emerged from the tomb (Colossians 2:11-15).

The outward expression we make is a public declaration to those who witness it, saying that you are now found in Christ. You have turned from your old self and are born again in and through Jesus. Having been raised to life, we now celebrate the triumph over those principalities and powers that were accomplished by Jesus for us.

We baptize to celebrate!

Acts is filled with the stories of people who came to believe the things the disciples were teaching, repented of their sins, and were baptized. Baptism always follows repentance, and is a mark on the new believer's life. Acts 16 tells the story of Lydia, how the Lord opened her heart to do what the disciples were teaching, and she and her household were baptized. She already had a faith in the living God, but the disciples had now come and shared about what Jesus had done and taught them. *"Upon hearing the Gospel and recognizing her need for Jesus, they were baptized"* (Acts 16:11-15).

Further down we see Paul and Silas confined to jail. They are in their cells singing and praying when an earthquake shook the foundations of the prison and the doors were opened. Interestingly, they remained in their cells. As a side note, had that been me, I would have taken that as God granting me freedom from my jailers and made my escape! The disciples did not do this however, and they remained. The jailer was fearful that he would lose his own life for having lost the prisoners, but Paul and Silas assured him, "*We are all here*" (Acts 16:25-28).

The jailer would have heard them singing and praying all night, and he now recognized the power of the true God. So in response, he asks what he must do to be saved.

The disciples taught the jailer and his household: believe in the Lord Jesus! And immediately he and all his family were baptized. The world was slowly being transformed by simply doing what Jesus had commanded.

We see time and again that after being taught of Jesus and making an admission of their need for Him, the disciples would baptize that person.

When a new believer comes into our lives, we don't have to wait for a pastor or a church service to baptize them. We can walk right into the water alongside them, and in the name of the Godhead we have the authority to baptize! All throughout the Word of God we see the action of baptism as one in which a person who has come into belief is submerged and pulled out of the water, representing what Jesus did when He went into the grave and rose again on the third day.

Disciples of Jesus will teach of the new life that He gives and baptize those who turn from death to life. There are a great many resources on the theology of baptism, but I would encourage you to turn to the Word of God and the examples we see there as the standard upon which we live out these practices of the Christian faith. Read through the book of Acts and see how obedience began to transform the world. The Word of God is a mighty yet frequently untapped resource for you to consume.

TEACH THEM

Believers who abstain from the Word of God either willfully or by simple neglect subject themselves to spiritual atrophy by choice.

Further on we will discuss the absolute necessity of knowing with accuracy the Word of God and all of its pages. I believe it is next to impossible for us to understand the nature and character of God if we do not digest His written words regularly. This is not only for our own spiritual sake, but if we are going to teach new disciples to observe all that Jesus has commanded us, we must have a functioning knowledge of the written word.

Without a certain depth in this area of our life, we absolutely cannot fully obey the Great Commission. The very nature of the Word is that It is living and active, able to teach us, rebuke us, and to cause growth in us. It gives us direct insight into God's will for us each and every day.

"Teaching them all that I have commanded you" is not just a job for your pastor. It is not a task that should be left solely to good books and time-tested theologians. It is not a task list item we accomplish by getting our family to attend Sunday service. It is a command to every believer that applies every day of the week.

If it is in your capacity, you should be both actively learning and teaching the Word and the commands of Jesus. Do this in your family by purposefully observing times of study together. Do this in your group of friends by discussing how the text confronts your sin in any given situation. Do this in your workplace by reading the Word publicly on your lunch break. I guarantee you will incite questions that will enable you to not only preach the Word but teach it as well.

Just as I was working on writing this today in a public place, a lady sat nearby to have her lunch. She asked what book I was reading. It was my Bible, laid open next to me as I worked.

Within moments, we were engaged in conversation about belief. She grew up in a home with a Catholic father and a Protestant mother, but she told me she knew very little of what either of those things meant.

We had a half-hour discussion about what it is that I believe. We discussed how being someone who believes in Jesus means that **He** accomplished the tasks needed for my salvation. We then talked about how almost every other religion requires you to engage in works to be saved. It is a list of check-boxes you have to hit in order to be assured of your eternity with God. Believing in Jesus means that **He** checked those boxes for us!

What an awesome conversation it was! I didn't lead her in a prayer to confess Christ, but I was able to simply teach her who Jesus is, what He did, and what He commands. We spoke of the cross and of what the Bible says about eternity.

Just by having my Bible out and visible. That's all it took.

In some parts of the world that is not an option. Some of the places I have gone do not allow you to openly display or read the Word. In those places it becomes especially vital that you build deep relationships with your neighbors and co-workers that will allow conversations in which you can point them to the teachings of Jesus.

Relationship is what restores us to God, and relationship is what enables you to teach the commands of Jesus. Build relationships so that you might teach His commands.

BEAR WITNESS

We have witnessed who Jesus is and what He has done, and we are sent to share that. In the Gospel of Luke, Jesus tells the disciples "*You are witnesses of these things*" (24:48). When someone has witnessed something worth knowing, they are compelled to speak of it.

We call those who attest to a crime in a court of law, "witnesses." People are either condemned to their rightful punishment or restored to freedom by both the word of witnesses and by physical evidence. It cannot be overstated that the word of a verifiable witness holds immense strength.

How do we, who are living on mission, verify this to those we encounter? In my own life, I bear witness to the change in my heart that happens when I'm in right relationship with God. I don't think the thoughts that my flesh would normally think, nor do I speak the things I would normally speak. These things in themselves bear witness to a changed life.

The evidence of a transformed life is perceivable to those around them. Your actions begin to look more like fruits of the Spirit rather than the fruits of your anger, of jealousy, of your family tree, or of your home environment.

When your life is transformed, you show clear evidence of it to those around you through your actions, attitudes, and responses. You begin to bear witness as the disciples did. They may have seen Jesus raised to life with their own eyes, but we get to see the fruit of a dead soul being brought to new life through the restoration of their soul to right relationship with God!

PREACH THE REMISSION OF SINS

"Jesus said to them again, "Peace be with you. As the Father has sent me, I also send you." After saying this, he breathed on them and said, "Receive the Holy Spirit. If you forgive the sins of any, they are forgiven them; if you retain the sins of any, they are retained.""
John 20:21-23

What does this actually mean? To preach the remission of sins? Are we actually sent out with the literal power to forgive people of their sins? How do we interpret this part of the Great Commission as people who believe that Jesus Himself is the only One who forgives sins?

What we see occurring in this text is the impartation of authority to the disciples who are being sent. They are being told first and foremost to receive the Holy Spirit, which will empower them to live in Christ. Secondly, He tells them that if they forgive anybody's sins, it is done. If they retain anybody's sins, they are retained.

This is a commonly confusing and often overlooked part of the Great Commission, so I would like to present two thoughts on this: how you and I are to live out this verse as individuals, and then together as the church.

As the Individual

This text is indeed a mandate for the collective Church, but consider this: we have been given roles individually in forgiveness and the restoration of relationships. I will address this in greater depth later, but I will touch on it briefly here because greater Gospel clarity precedes greater Gospel impact as we prepare to live on mission.

It is of absolute importance that we work on maintaining healthy relationships in the body of Christ, for the enemy works daily to disrupt our families, friendships, and marriages.

Consider your interpersonal relationships through the lens of this command. If you have been wronged or sinned against, you personally bear the weight of responsibility to make the choice of forgiveness or of holding a grudge. Freedom in Christ truly comes through forgiveness.

In this command from Jesus as He sends disciples, it says He breathes on them, telling them to receive the Holy Spirit. Then He says that if we forgive the sins of any, they are forgiven. If we retain (hold onto) those sins, they are retained.

I imagine you could easily think of some person who has sinned against you to which you are retaining their sin. You refuse to let it go. Perhaps you have told the person you forgive them, but internally you still wage war with the fact that they have wronged you.

Are you holding onto the sins of another person? Has what they did to you driven a wedge into your relationship? Are you being separated from somebody because you're retaining their wrongs against you?

Or are you acting as Christ did? Who, though we wrong Him daily, has forgiven our sins completely. He could have chosen to retain those sins against us, but instead, through grace, we are forgiven! If you choose to forgive them of their sin against you, you will live a much more joyful life, being given the fullness of joy that is assured us when we live as Christ intends.

As the Church

"We don't retain sins, but we collectively declare the condition on which sins are remitted, and with the plenary powers of an ambassador pronounces their remission or retention."

- G.H. Trench

As Evangelical Christians, we have zero power to forgive humanity of their sins and restore them to right relationship with God. Yet we see this exemplified in the Catholic world as a core part of their beliefs. The task is given to clergy to assign penance and forgive those who have sinned, acting as a bridge between man and God. Under the New Covenant, there is no scriptural allowance for this practice within the written Word of God.

It is **solely** by the work of Jesus that we have forgiveness. We go to the Father through Him. Humans have tried for years to take the role of Christ upon ourselves inside our churches and religions. We create mandates or routes to forgiveness that exclude the work of Christ by putting conditions upon the sinner to be forgiven.

What G.H. Trench is saying in the quote above is that we, as the Church, have been imparted with the authority to tell the world how sins are indeed forgiven. As an ambassador would speak on his leader's behalf with undisputed authority, we are speaking to address the sins of the world on behalf of God. We are not giving or withholding salvation, as that role belongs solely to God. Our objective is to bring others towards a correct knowledge of God. Jesus says we (the believer) are to be teaching them—both those who do not yet believe, and those who have come into belief—all that He has commanded us.

To me, this is an example of the proverbial saying in its perfect place: "You can lead a horse to water, but you can't make it drink."

Our job is to profess Christ, tell how sin separates us from

God, and point them to forgiveness. If a believer refuses to repent of their sin and continues to live in it within the church after we biblically confront them, as taught to us in Matthew 18, we are told to put that person out of the assembly. This is not something we should do out of spite or hatred—as the world likes to claim we are doing by labeling Christians with all kinds of phobias and "isms"—but rather we do this out of obedience to the teachings of the Word.

1 Corinthians 5 addresses sexual immorality that was occurring within the church. Note that last part, "**in the church**." Paul says that this person within the church living in unrepentant sin is to literally be "*delivered to Satan for the destruction of the flesh, that his spirit may be saved in the day of the Lord Jesus*" (1 Corinthians 5:5).

Wow, what a sentence.

Let's dig into this verse. Someone in the church is sleeping with their father's wife. This relationship is a perversion of God's intended design for marriage and a resistance to the sexual ethic laid out by God. It is a sin. This person is in defiance of correction and is choosing to continue in sin. They are assumed to be a believer, or Paul would not address it in this way. Why do we know that? Because the very next section of his letter states that he wants believers to be keeping company with sexually immoral people. What?!

He says of unbelievers, "*What have I to do with judging those who also are outside? Do you not judge those who are inside? But those who are outside God judges*" (1 Corinthians 5:12-13).

To shorten it up, Paul says that we should absolutely be associating ourselves with unbelievers. But those who do not have a relationship with Jesus are not held to the same moral standard as those who claim to be in right relationship with God, and are therefore a part of the Body.

Jesus himself associated with the most sinful persons of His day. Prostitutes and tax collectors were those He kept company with. His example is that we be with them in relationship. In what other way will we be able to share the hope of the Gospel with them?

When a person has come into relationship with Jesus and has decided to engage in the community of the Church, they are supposed to submit themselves to the accountability of the Word of God alongside the people of God.

The Word will always confront our sin. Someone growing in spiritual maturity will allow that confrontation to occur and desire to step forward in their walk with Christ. Paul is addressing someone here who is choosing to live outside the accountability of the Church and the moral standard of God. Once addressed and found unwilling to change, Paul says that we are to—through the power of our Lord Jesus Christ—deliver that person to satan for the destruction of the flesh, that his spirit may be saved in the day of the Lord.

Once we have dealt with a believer living in unrepentant

sin with love and in the correct Biblical format, we are then to trust God with their soul. Because the Holy Spirit is active in them, we can be assured that He is doing His job of conviction as we know He does (John 16). Our job is to address the sin Biblically, be obedient to the Word in our actions (which we **have** control over) and trust God to do the work in their heart (which we **do not** have control over). Obedience is our job.

We cannot forgive people of their sins. We can live alongside them, working together as we fail and fall, aiming to hold each other accountable and to grow together as the body into maturity. But, when the Church is confronted by glaring sin that separates us from God, we do have the power to authoritatively call that out. When someone walks without repentance in sin, we are able to tell them that they are giving up the forgiveness of Christ in favor of their sinful identity.

Our job as disciples is to preach the forgiveness of sin and to inform of the consequence of sin: death.

PAUL'S INSTRUCTIONS

It is worth our time also to examine some quick thoughts on discipleship from the life of Paul. We will examine more from him later on as we look at how to live out the mission once we've prepared for it. For now let's take a look at this short scripture.

Paul tells the church in Corinth to **"Imitate me, as I also imitate Christ"** (1 Corinthians 11:1). He understood that his job as a disciple was to imitate Christ. And his job as a disciple maker was to teach other people to imitate Christ in turn. He obviously was a broken human as you and I are, so he failed frequently. Yet he told the believers to imitate himself.

Some have noted what a high level of arrogance this man must have had to make such a bold statement! On the contrary, I believe Paul said this because he wanted them to imitate his repentance after failure. We must learn to live lives in constant surrender and repentance amidst our greatest weakness.

Paul wanted them to imitate him as he continued learning the Gospel more and more. Paul wanted them to imitate Christ. The church didn't know how to do a lot of the "christian things" yet, but Paul could show them how to live out their faith as he walked it out himself.

As Paul gets older and understands grace all the more, he claims how great a sinner he is. Every time we see Paul talk about his sin, he claims to be an even worse sinner than the last time! Paul wasn't getting mixed up in more sinful natures. Rather, he was growing to understand Jesus more deeply. This drove him to recognize just how much of sinner he was and how great the grace of God proved to be.

I insist on this principle: **we cannot obediently live out our Christian faith without stepping into the work of mak-**

ing disciples. Growing into a deeper spiritual maturity glorifies God in our lives and causes us to point others towards the same. This is the job of the Church: to preach the Good News and make disciples.

WAIT

If we've been given the power of the Holy Spirit when we begin a relationship with Jesus and we are sent, why does Jesus tell the disciples to wait? What purpose was their waiting in Jerusalem supposed to accomplish? If we have the Holy Spirit, why wait for more of it?

Here we reach a rather sharp divide between those of Christian faith who believe that there are to be two separate "encounters" with the Holy Spirit. The indwelling of the Spirit at salvation, and the baptism or "filling" of the Holy Spirit that occurs when given a second "surge" of power. Often this is considered to be evidenced by language gifts (speaking in tongues) or the empowerment for specific gifts such as healing or the prophetic.

Rather than divide this conversation further or take a polarized stance, I want to look at the value of waiting as Jesus instructed them. I want to highlight the evidences that occurred when they obeyed the specific command to wait.

The direct result of the disciples waiting in Jerusalem led

to the fulfillment of the prophecy we read in Joel 2:32: "...*there will be an escape for those on Mount Zion and in Jerusalem.*"

This moment resulted in thousands upon thousands of people coming to Christ. From there the Church began to grow and the work of the Gospel took root. Perhaps that was the simple reason Jesus said to wait! It was His will that Jerusalem would see this outpouring of the Spirit and for the disciples be together in unity for that specific moment.

They were to bear witness to what had occurred and to proclaim the Gospel. What could have been the result if they had scattered to their homes and various workplaces once He ascended? They may have all been filled with the Spirit, but look at the magnificent work of Jesus in drawing people to God when they (the disciples) were together for this moment.

God was glorified, the Church was edified, and the lost were saved. The disciples' job was obedience; that is why they needed to stay in Jerusalem.

In what areas of your life are you being told to wait right now? Be obedient in that time. Remain in close community with other believers whom you can encounter God with, and wait for the revelation of His power in your life.

Part One: Understanding

THE PROMISE OF THE HOLY SPIRIT

The promises of God are sure, and have never been in question. Throughout the Old Testament we see His promises delivered upon, even in those who in a moment of despair felt abandoned. We, who know the end of their stories, often look and say, "Why didn't you trust God, you fool! Clearly He was working on your behalf!"

It is easy for us to say that now because we know He did indeed follow through on His promise.

The promises of God to Abraham, made through the covenants into which they entered, have been delivered upon. In fact, they still are! I say this to point out that in our limited perspective, we ought to stand on the authority of knowing that God always has and always will continue to deliver on His promises.

Every infallible word we have of promise in the Bible remains true today. When we examine Jesus' words as He sends the disciples on mission, we can with full assurance expect those words to be upheld for all time.

> *I am sending you what my Father promised. As for you, stay in the city until you are empowered as from on high.*
> Luke 24:49

The promise of the Father is the promise of a Helper. We now experience this Helper as the person of the Holy Spirit. We could spend a great many chapters on the roles and the impact of the Holy Spirit in our lives. For our purposes today however, we will examine only a few of His roles. I encourage you to seek more clarity on the work of the Spirit in your life.

It seems that **sometimes we become so distracted with what we hope the Holy Spirit might do that we often forget what He is doing currently.** Our hopes of seeing the miraculous occur, or of "spontaneously fantastic worship services," can sometimes overshadow the things He is actively doing in our lives. We need to understand that a massive part of the

Holy Spirit's role in our lives is to empower us for the sake of mission.

He does do miracles, revealing Himself both to us and to those around us in unique and unimaginable ways. When we read the Word of God we see that when the Holy Spirit acts to empower the believer, it is for the glory of God and the purpose of drawing people **to** Jesus. It is not for our enjoyment or entertainment.

When you are spiritually mature, **you do not need special moments in a worship service to provide emotional evidence that God indeed loves you.** There is an absolute greatness of joy and assurance we feel when He does reveal Himself to us in those moments. Be assured, I do not diminish those moments for a second. **If we rightly understand the job of the Holy Spirit, then we would be just as content to live out our mundane days with as much joy and assurance as days in which we experience the miraculous.**

If we live our lives in search of spiritually-climactic moments, we fail to enjoy the stability of God's steadfastness. There is often a lack of depth of spiritual maturity in a person chasing those feelings. Most of the stories we read about in the hall of Faith (Hebrews 11) highlight a moment in those people's lives in which God did something extravagant.

In our ability to trust God through the mundane, we can see His character with a clearer and more accurate understanding.

Part One: Understanding

Those of us who become distracted or disappointed by the lack of the miraculous or spoken gifts have missed the Holy Spirit's core duties in our lives. His role is to point us to God, through Jesus. His role is to convict us of our sin, drawing us towards a depth which is solely accomplished through repentance.

Let's examine this moment in scripture once more:

> *While he was with them, he commanded them not to leave Jerusalem, but to wait for the Father's promise. "Which," he said, "you have heard me speak about; for John baptized with water, but you will be baptized with the Holy Spirit in a few days." So when they had come together, they asked him, "Lord, are you restoring the kingdom to Israel at this time?" He said to them, "It is not for you to know times or periods that the Father has set by his own authority. But you will receive power when the Holy Spirit has come on you, and you will be my witnesses in Jerusalem, in all Judea and Samaria, and to the ends of the earth.*
> Acts 1:4-8

The Holy Spirit fell on those at the time of Pentecost with a magnificent power that transformed people. It literally transformed the world. It set the course of growth for the Church that we know today. The promise of the power and guidance of the Holy Spirit demands our thankfulness for His involvement in our life, no matter how the gifts manifest in us.

Though we could spend hours on this topic alone, we will focus only on just three things that are a result of His promise of the Holy Spirit.

HE WILL BE WITH US

"And remember, I am with you always, to the end of the age."
Matthew 28:20

If no other promise mattered today, this is what we can stand on. Christ assures us that He will be with us. Do you realize that God, the Creator of the universe and all its marvels, the One who knows every moment of your life and every decision you will make, has promised to be with you until the end of the age?

He has delivered on this promise by sending us Jesus. Then, He doubled-down on that promise by sending the Holy Spirit, so that we would never be physically without the presence of God in our daily lives!

The mature believer now can stand on this promise with such confidence and joy. When grasped fully, this promise has the ability to sustain them through both the highest and lowest moments of their lives.

When we go into our work day dreading customers or the attitude of our co-worker, remember He is with us. When we encounter the death of a loved one in our life and have only tears to express our pain, He is with us. When we celebrate the greatest moments in our life, He is with us! When we reel from an unexpected tragedy, He is with us.

The believer must stand on this promise that He is with us, even when we don't perceive that He is. When we lose sight of this truth and forget His steadfastness, we feel the agony of the broken human life at its most severe.

All I could hope for in this short section of my writing is that you would contemplate this reality. Please examine the Word of God for yourself and conclude it to be true. **He is Lord, and He remains with you always.**

The disciple today who is assured of this promise will be effective throughout the whole of their life. No circumstance they encounter will be without this knowledge of Him. People watching you live out your life will observe as you stand on these promises. The simplicity of Jesus' statement should cause us to run towards the task set before us with joy, knowing that He is indeed with us.

DON'T GET DISTRACTED

I'm always amazed when I read and see how the disciples were so easily distracted and shortsighted. I'm certain I show the same immaturity and shortsightedness daily. Consider this part of the text:

> *So when they had come together, they asked him, "Lord, are you restoring the kingdom to Israel at this time?" He said to them, "It is not for you to know times or periods that the Father has set by his own authority. But you will receive power when the Holy Spirit has come on you, and you will be my witnesses in Jerusalem, in all Judea and Samaria, and to the ends of the earth."*
> Acts 1:6-8

Jesus had just commissioned them and had promised them His Spirit. Their first response is to ask about what they hoped to see in that moment. How many times has the Lord given me a command only to have me ask a nearsighted question, forgetting that He is Lord over all time?

In this question from the disciples we see them asking about the kingdom they lived in for the moment. Jesus is focused on the eternal Kingdom. The takeaway: our vision is shortsighted, but His is forever.

Keep your focus on the long view, aiming to have your perspective aligned to match that of Christ.

The disciples wanted to know if He would restore the kingdom of Israel in their lifetime. His response is patient and clear; "*It is not for you to know times or seasons which the Father has put in His own authority. But...*"

I love that but. He corrects them, and realigns their focus. "*But you shall receive power.*" We don't need to know the time, but we are promised power sufficient for it.

Don't get distracted by what you hope to see happen in the here and now. Rather, empowered by the Holy Spirit, shift your focus onto Jesus, the Author and Finisher of your faith.

THERE WILL BE SIGNS

I believe that the gifts are for today. That may be a polarizing statement in some circles, but I feel it is one I can make with great conviction and confidence. I have seen with my own eyes the power of God as He has miraculously healed people we have prayed for in the moment we uttered the prayer. I have seen people speak in tongues that they would have never known. I have seen the power of God manifest in ways I cannot describe.

Perhaps you've seen something you cannot describe. Perhaps you've been sitting on the fence and you're not sure if you believe that God's Spirit is active in these ways today. I would challenge you to ask God to reveal Himself to you in these things. I'm confident He will surprise you.

What matters, though, is that every single time I've seen the gifts be exercised, it has been for God's glory. Nothing else. It's not for my joy, nor for my fulfillment, but solely for the glory of God. Every time I've seen the gifts of God manifest in a scriptural way, I've witnessed people come to know or understand the Gospel. I believe that the gifts of God are for the glory of God, and that we should joyfully seek them together.

Jesus promised we would see His power as we walk with the Spirit on mission. What I do **not** want is for us to get hung up on the way or the time that gifts manifest, nor to be so distracted by the gifts themselves that we lose our understanding of their purpose.

We know the Spirit gives the gifts in His timing, and as He sees fit. A less frequently observed reality is that sometimes the gifts are for a season. Our job is not to question the gifts, or their timing, but to walk in the promised power of the Holy Spirit.

I heard it said so plainly once by a missionary named Jason Biel: **"Any believer could potentially operate in any gift at any given time."**

You would think that this simple truth would not come as a surprise. However, many believers have developed a bit of misunderstanding in this area. If the Holy Spirit is sovereign enough to distribute the gifts, then He is also able to restrict their movement in people's lives.

THEIR DIVERSITY

> *"Now there are different gifts, but the same Spirit. There are different ministries, but the same Lord. And there are different activities, but the same God works all of them in each person."*
>
> 1 Corinthians 12:4-6

Paul emphasizes that the signs and gifts accompanying the indwelling of the Spirit are given by and for the glory of God.

He points out that there are different gifts, ministries, and activities. But he starts the whole text keeping our perspective aligned correctly. They come from **one Spirit.**

Sometimes in our Christian communities, we become jealous when we see certain gifts being either given or expressed in other parts of the church. This is an unhealthy response to God's design for humanity. We are in fact given different roles in life. As the Church, we should celebrate this instead of lament it!

If all of the gifts are coming from one Spirit, then despite their diversity, they will always point to one thing: unity. No portion of the Church functioning in its gifts should cause division in another part of the body. If division is the result of the Spirit's gifts and signs, it is more likely a misappropriation of our emotions and response than a misuse of the gift itself.

Segments of the Evangelical Church have become fractured over the last thousand years. Often these divisions have occurred because of different interpretations of how the gifts ought to be expressed. The longer I have traveled and the more of the global Church I've had the chance to see, the less concerned I become with how local bodies are expressing these things.

Unless it is completely and blatantly anti-Gospel, and the Spirit Himself is setting off discernment alarms within us, we ought to trust that God (in His sovereignty) will work these things out amongst His followers.

If God has put you in a position to speak into these situations, seek unity instead of division. Point people back to Jesus, let the Holy Spirit do the convicting, and use the gifts He has endowed you with to grow the Church. There is one Spirit, and He is way better at His job than we are.

THEIR PURPOSE

"A manifestation of the Spirit is given to each person for the common good..."

1 Corinthians 12:7

The reason the Spirit enables us to operate in gifts and signs is not for personal pleasure or entertainment, nor simply for personal edification. Rather, it is for the profit of the Body (the global Church) and for the revelation of who Jesus is to the lost.

Yes, your faith is emboldened when you see the gifts of the Spirit in your own life, but the overarching purpose in the acts of God is the glory of God. We must not forget this.

Becoming a person who will affect change in the world means we realize it is not us impacting the world with our own abilities and strengths, but the Spirit of God moving in and through us.

The manifestation of the Spirit is given to each of us, for the sake of all of us. We're built up together into a stronger expression of the Church when we operate independently and cooperatively as the Spirit guides us in our action.

SIGNS AND FRUIT

Some of the Spirit's gifts will bewilder us when we see them occur, like the ones we're going to read about in the book of Mark in the next section.

Other gifts should be naturally-occurring in us as we grow in spiritual maturity. Those gifts of the Spirit are called fruits. Paul gives us a clear picture of what those are in Galatians 5:22-23:

"But the fruit of the Spirit is love, joy, peace, patience, kindness, goodness, faithfulness, gentleness, and self-control. The law is not against such things."

Fruits emerge from within us to show the power of God as the Spirit transforms the way we act and re-act. Signs happen through us to show the power of God as we live our lives pointing others toward Him. Do you see the common goal of them all?

Ultimately, all of the signs and gifts we see manifest in our lives attest to the majesty and power of God as He transforms us.

Part One: Understanding

JESUS EXPLAINS GIFTS

We are told by Jesus that those who follow Him will have signs that accompany them. In Mark we read:

> *And these signs will accompany those who believe: In my name they will drive out demons; they will speak in new tongues; they will pick up snakes; if they should drink anything deadly, it will not harm them; they will lay hands on the sick, and they will get well.*
> *Mark 16:17-18*

We are given an incredible level of authority over the enemy and the world we live in. However, we must realize that it is only in His name and by His power that any of these authorities can be exercised. One singular God has given these things, and one Spirit is enabling them.

As Jesus explains the signs that will follow His believers, He is expressing an authority which only comes through our relationship with Him. These signs are an outward expression of the authority of God being revealed to and through His people.

Be it driving out demons, surviving miraculously, or healing the sick, we see the evidence of God's authority imparted to us. To see these expressed in our lives, we must be living in accordance with the Spirit of God, obeying His word, and living in close relationship with Him.

In doing this we have the confidence that any of the spiritual gifts described here may in fact be manifested in our own lives, at any given time the Spirit wills it. When they occur, God is made more magnificent in the eyes of the world.

PAUL EXPLAINS GIFTS

> To one is given a message of wisdom through the Spirit, to another, a message of knowledge by the same Spirit, to another, faith by the same Spirit, to another, gifts of healing by the one Spirit, to another, the performing of miracles, to another, prophecy, to another, distin-

> *guishing between spirits, to another, different kinds of tongues, to another, interpretation of tongues.*
> 1 Corinthians 12:8-10

We do not all need nor get the same gifts. Imagine the chaos and frustration if one gift was singularly manifested by itself in a community, with no other gifts or roles being employed. It would be highly ineffective.

As a simple example: if every single person in your portion of the Church body was incredibly good at hosting a gathering, but nobody was capable of leading a gathering, you would all just stand around eating good food waiting for something to happen. **Things are a mess when everybody does the same thing.**

We need the diversity and variety of gifts that God gives for a healthy Body to exist. Paul addresses this also in Ephesians four when he teaches that there are different leadership roles in the Body of Christ to be filled. We need them **all** so that we can grow together in spiritual maturity and reach the lost.

> *And he himself gave some to be apostles, some prophets, some evangelists, some pastors and teachers, to equip the saints for the work of ministry, to build up the body of Christ, until we all reach unity in the faith and in the knowledge of God's Son, growing into maturity with a*

> *stature measured by Christ's fullness. Then we will no longer be little children, tossed by the waves and blown around by every wind of teaching, by human cunning with cleverness in the techniques of deceit.*
> Ephesians 4:11-15

To understand what the gifts are, we need to understand the One who gives them first. The Spirit of God is the person of God living in us, directing us to do good works and to be in closeness of relationship with the Father through Jesus. Any gift He gives will be aiming to accomplish those purposes. To know and understand the purposes of God, we must first understand the heart of God. His heart is for the lost. His heart is for the unification of the divided. The gifts and their outward manifestations will aim for these things. The gifts are exactly that: gifts from God, to His people, for His purpose.

Many persons, with far more wisdom than I have made more in depth expositions of these passages. So for simplicity's sake, we will just focus on how the gifts are astoundingly powerful, and will transform the lives of those who witness them.

You will be amazed at how the Spirit will work through you over the course of your life if you seek Him and let the Spirit work as He wills for His glory. My encouragement to you is not to seek the gifts first however; seek Jesus first.

THE WHEN AND THE WHERE

> *One and the same Spirit is active in all these, distributing to each person as he wills. For just as the body is one and has many parts, and all the parts of that body, though many, are one body—so also is Christ.*
> 1 Corinthians 12:11-12

I'll start with this thought: we probably don't need to concern ourselves quite as much as we do, with the when and where these happen. As I aforementioned, if we seek Jesus first we will see the gifts pointing people to God.

Some segments of the Christian church have become so focused on the here and now, that they forget the Spirit is capable of good timing. The Spirit is much better timed than you or I. Let's trust Him.

This part of the Bible tells us that though we may seek the gifts—which is not wrong to do—we need to fully trust that the Spirit will distribute them as He sees fit. We are not the ones to tell the Spirit how and when, but rather we trust God's sovereignty on these issues.

So, if the Spirit distributes them as He wills to whom He wills, we don't need to be so concerned if we are without a particular gifting. If He sees fit and it will bring absolute glory to God in that moment, He can enable you to walk in it!

I know far too many believers who have lived their lives

feeling as failures because they have not yet spoken in other tongues. I know believers who have listened to blatant lies of the enemy telling them they are not worthy of operating in the gifts because of their sins.

Sin separates us from God, yes. But if you have been cleansed by the blood of Jesus and now live as a redeemed person, then your sins have been forgiven. Yes, we do need to confess our sins daily as we fail. The fact that you feel convicted into confessing your sins reveals that you in fact have the Holy Spirit living in you, drawing you back into healthy relationship with God! That's His job (John 16).

If you do not have the gift you desire or long for, then simply ask God. Matthew 7 says that we can ask, seek, and knock. God truly desires that we function as a part of the body, operating in the gifts He desires for us.

Take the pressure off of yourself.

If you are in right relationship with God and you have need of a specific gift in a certain time or place, trust that He will give it to you! It could be for one moment.

I have never operated throughout my life as one with the gift of seeing people healed, but I could list a number of times in my life that I felt a strong conviction to pray for a sick person and have seen them healed before my own eyes. In those moments the will of God was the glory of God through those works. He appropriated as He saw fit to do those works.

Trust God, seek Jesus, and walk in the faith that you have.

Then you will begin to operate fully in your gifts as the Spirit sees fit.

THE GREATEST GIFT: LOVE

Let's skip down a few verses and look at 1 Corinthians 13. Paul continues his address on the operation of the gifts within the Church, speaking to the entirety of the Body, not just to those who operate in or seek certain gifts:

> *If I speak human or angelic tongues but do not have love, I am a noisy gong or a clanging cymbal. If I have the gift of prophecy and understand all mysteries and all knowledge, and if I have all faith so that I can move mountains but do not have love, I am nothing. And if I give away all my possessions, and if I give over my body in order to boast but do not have love, I gain nothing.*
> *1 Corinthians 13:1-3*

Paul clearly states the priority here: if we have all these gifts and operate in them fully, but we do not have love, then we are using the gifts worthlessly.

He says if we speak in tongues, if we operate in the prophetic, if we have enormous faith and have given away all of our belongings, we still can end up having profited nothing.

This is such a convicting scripture to me. How many times do I focus my efforts on perfecting my talents or gifts for the sake of the Body, yet overlook the simplest ways I could love those I interact with daily?

It is far too easy for me to become focused on doing things for the Gospel that I forget the simplicity of the Gospel. We love because He first loved us!

What is the point of any gifting if we overlook love? **Without love for the lost, our evangelistic efforts are simply dead works.** If I preach the Gospel to far off countries but have not developed a love for the people themselves who God sent His son Jesus for, then my efforts are simply that: efforts.

God can work through your efforts, bringing people to Him through the spoken words of the Gospel that you proclaim, but Paul is saying that if you do any of these things without love, it profits you nothing.

Careful now, because suddenly we've made this about what it profits us. This can be slightly confusing. Let's not become distracted, but rather adjust the lens back enough to view the full picture.

God's desire is that you walk in the fullness of joy that He intended for you. Your relationship with Jesus accomplishes this. John Piper regularly says, "*God is most glorified in us when we are most satisfied in Him.*"

He gets the glory when we are operating out of a transformed heart. It profits me nothing if I do the gifts without love, because my heart is clearly not operating from a transformed spot. If Jesus has transformed me, I have come to understand God's love in a deeper way. Now, I want to operate in the gifts (evangelism for example) because I want to see God made known to the lost.

If this is motivated by love, it is a reflection of my new heart having been transformed by Jesus. If this is motivated by any other thing, it is done as works. It becomes something I am doing because I feel God requires it for me to be fully loved. It can quickly become a salvation response based on my good works, not the love of God. We must love others if we are to operate in the works of the Spirit.

THE CHURCH WILL GROW

> *But you will receive power when the Holy Spirit has come on you, and you will be my witnesses in Jerusalem, in all Judea and Samaria, and to the ends of the earth.*
> Acts 1:8

The growth of the global Church will be the inevitable result of our bearing witness to and preaching of the Gospel. The signs which accompany a healthy community teaching Jesus will be self-evident among the Church and to those watching

Part One: Understanding

in the world.

All throughout Acts and into today, we see that healthy churches create disciples, disciples share and teach the Gospel, and the church experiences growth. We begin where we are, loving those closest to us in our daily activities and sharing the Gospel with them. Then, as the church expands, we see it begin to reach outward.

When Jesus told them to stay in Jerusalem, we saw the Church grow in number. It grew into Judea, spread into Samaria, and praise God, today we are seeing the Gospel preached to the literal ends of the earth.

This type of growth doesn't happen accidentally. The growth of the Church began as it was persecuted and dispersed throughout the region. From there we see different types of growth happen. Internally, as God's plan started being intentionally executed, and through the choices of His people responding to the Gospel, traveling and sharing Jesus.

> *So the Lord Jesus, after speaking to them, was taken up into heaven and sat down at the right hand of God. And they went out and preached everywhere, while the Lord worked with them and confirmed the word by the accompanying signs.*
> *Mark 16:19-20*

The Lord was working with early believers to confirm His

Word through signs. The disciples went and preached, and the Lord confirmed His Word among His people.

Remember, we are not preaching as people without authority. The Lord will stir the hearts of those who hear and draw them unto Himself. He will confirm the Word as we obediently fulfill the command to go and preach it.

We must trust that His confirmation will be sufficient. Again, our job is solely obedience.

TRANSFORMED PEOPLE CHANGE THE WAY THEY LIVE

> *With many other words he testified and strongly urged them, saying, "Be saved from this corrupt generation!" So those who accepted his message were baptized, and that day about three thousand people were added to them. They devoted themselves to the apostles' teaching, to the fellowship, to the breaking of bread, and to prayer. Everyone was filled with awe, and many wonders and signs were being performed through the apostles. Now all the believers were together and held all things in common. They sold their possessions and property and distributed the proceeds to all, as any had need. Every day they devoted themselves to meeting together in the temple, and broke bread from house*

Part One: Understanding

> to house. They ate their food with joyful and sincere hearts, praising God and enjoying the favor of all the people. Every day the Lord added to their number those who were being saved.
> Acts 2:40-47

When the three thousand new believers joined the Church, there was evidence of transformation in their lives. Sinful, selfish people don't generally do the things we just read about without another compulsion such as governmental influence.

The people described in Acts 2 are people who desired earnestly for the good of each other and for the salvation of the lost.

"*They devoted themselves to the apostles' teaching, to the fellowship, to the breaking of bread, and to prayer.*" (verse 42). They actively became the Church! They continued the study of the Word and purposefully stayed in relationship with each other.

Look at the result of this unity within the early Church: more growth! "*All who believed were together, and had all things in common*" (verse 45). The Church upheld one another with their belongings and possessions.

Their perspective on what they owned shifted when their perspective on eternity changed.

The result of a changed perspective on eternity created a type of absurd generosity, not commonly known in the world today. It says they sold belongings and ensured that everyone had what they needed.

Political structures and governments have been trying to duplicate this system for thousands of years. It rarely works, however, because its motivation is temporal, not eternal. When you have only a lifetime to acquire and use your wealth, you have very little motivation to share it.

When your perspective is changed and you realize you have an eternity with the One who created all things, you realize you have a much shorter need for the things you earn in this life.

Gospel transformation changes your perspective on everything you do. We, being the Church, should give generously because we are motivated by the love we discussed a few pages back in 1 Corinthians 13.

The result of disciples living on mission will be the growth of the Church. Growth will occur locally as new believers become a part, and globally as those called to travel for the sake of the Gospel undertake their calling.

WHAT'S THE PROOF?

Jesus is real.

I can say with authority that Jesus is real because He has literally changed my life. As we have already discussed, the external evidence of His authority comes in the form of a transformation of my nature.

For some people, however, that weight of evidence just doesn't cut it. Some people we encounter will require a much more logical, scientific evidence of the person of Jesus.

That evidence exists, and we just need to know how to point people to it. There are a great many resources devoted to proving the life, resurrection, and ascension of Jesus. The Word of God has evidences of its validity that reach far beyond what most people are aware of.

If we are to point people effectively to Jesus, we should be willing and ready to make a factual proof of His personhood and nature. Invest time into learning these things. But my encouragement to you today is that we should let our changed lives be the evidentiary facts that express these proofs to the world. The power of personal testimony holds more weight as a proof than you can imagine.

Over the millennia a great many persons have set out to disprove the validity of the Word only to end up meeting Jesus, having their lives changed by the very thing they set out to disprove.

Sadly, some will just never believe. They choose to ignore the physical proofs or have hardened their hearts against God. Throughout the world many of the people I've met who claim to be atheist or agnostic have a skewed version of what that even means. They claim disbelief, but if you begin to ask what or why they believe (or do not believe), you will often find an expressed disappointment in their expectations of God.

I remember one such person my band met in France. We were sharing the Gospel in the city center, playing music and inviting people into conversations. This particular person said he had no faith, but after a few moments of conversation he told us he did still in fact believe that God was real. He was disappointed because God didn't heal his grandma who had died of cancer.

Often one's claim of disbelief only serves to mask their hardened heart. Sharing the proof and evidences in your own life, along with the living and active Word of God, can confront a hardened heart with truth in such a way as to liberate their unbelief.

I've encountered many people who simply dispute the existence of God or the validity of the Word of God because they claim it contradicts itself. Their misunderstanding of Gospel truths cause them to view it from a skewed perspective.

This should not surprise us! Jesus knew that people would not believe. Paul addressed this when he spoke to the church

Part One: Understanding

in Corinth. In 1 Corinthians, he pens what I feel may be some of his most powerful words:

"For the word of the cross is foolishness to those who are perishing, but it is the power of God to us who are being saved" (1 Corinthians 1:18).

Note the difference between the two types of people: belief. To those who have not heard or made a choice not to believe, the Word seems foolish. Remember in the beginning of this book how we discussed that our first task is belief?

Everything about our relationship with God takes form after we choose to believe in who He is. Upon that transformation, your faith literally opens your eyes to truths that before were hidden. The Word of God as a completed textual work is no small accomplishment that could have been logically assembled as it was.

Across three continents, over fifteen hundred years, more than forty persons wrote their accounts of historical lineage, of prophecy, and of Jesus. They had no modern technologies to assist them in getting the story right. They could not correspond to ensure accuracy. The Holy Spirit Himself inspired the writers, ensuring that the origin of the text did indeed come from one person: God Himself.

Today, **the simplest proof you can show a skeptic is your obedience to the call and your changed life through Jesus.**

Personally, I'm a poor debater. I acknowledge I have very slow wit and response in a back-and-forth, debate-style conversation. But what I do have and know is that Jesus changed my life. The evidential proof is in my capacity to forgive when I've been wronged, which is obviously not my normal compulsory response! There are a great many studies and confirmations of the validity of the Word of God, but your assent in sharing the Gospel is that it has changed you.

The Word has stood the test of time and will continue to stand until the very return of Jesus Himself. We can be sure that It is self-sufficient to stand against Its fiercest critics, because It is the very written Word of the Creator God Himself.

I marvel at the gifted people who can quickly defend It, both critically and with well-thought-out words and academic insight. If that is you, then be obedient to that call and operate in your gifting in love. If it is not you, your job again is obedience. Obey the commands and instructions of the Gospel to evidence the person of Jesus to those you live and work alongside. Your transformed life, the manner in which you love them despite their shortcomings, and your continual growth will become a sufficient proof.

Part Two: Preparing

PART TWO.

PREPARING TO LIVE ON MISSION

AM I A MISSIONARY?

If we now have established a clearer understanding of the mission and its commands, then the next thing to ask is "Who among us is qualified and sent?"

The short answer: every single one of us who believe.

Some of us will indeed be called and capable of more specific things, but we don't have to question the fact that each and every Bible-believing Christian has the call of God on their life to live out His mission. The entire last section on understanding our mission in Christ should have affirmed this to be true.

We are both qualified and empowered by the Father. We are not qualified for the overall mission by anything we do or accomplish. Some of us may have more qualification and capability to serve in various methods than others, but **the qualifier of the believer is the Creator.** Some of us may, over the course of our lives, develop capacities or abilities that enable us to do mission in unique or more difficult environments, but that in itself is not the sole qualification for mission.

I want to affirm that there is a specific preparation for us to undertake if we are to impart the Gospel-founded change we wish to see in the world.

Later on in these pages, we will specifically address the difference between mission and method, in which I believe many missionaries and believers misappropriate their passions.

I hope that you have read the many stories of God using feeble and weak people throughout the Bible. I'm certain you've even heard the stories of famous achievers in our modern world who were disqualified at a young age. The world loves to root for the underdog, cheering them on to great success through their accomplishments and ingenuity.

Yes. You are indeed called to mission.

Exactly how and where you do mission may not be so clear to you. However, the need for your obedience is urgent.

GENERAL CALLINGS

We have already looked at how God gives specific spiritual gifts to some and not to others. It is not something for us to stress over. The people that Paul speaks about in Ephesians 4 are ones set apart for a particular work inside the Church, which are specific callings.

The rest of us — who are living out our lives without a pull toward pastoral ministry, or overseas missions — have the mandate to live out what we call "general callings." Basically, these would be anything taught to us by the Word of God and directed to every believer. The things which have been taught to the Church and are commanded by Jesus as He walked the earth are the things which you are called to.

If Jesus commanded it, you do it. Live a life that glorifies God and fulfills the Great Commission by simply being obedient to the directives of God.

Be aware, listen to the voice of His Spirit as He guides you into truth, affirm those truths are indeed scriptural, and then do them. These same steps are to be applied whether you are a lead pastor or a middle school student.

If it's commanded in the Bible, it's a statement intended to be followed. This is a general calling for all believers. Our job, once again, is obedience.

SPECIFIC CALLINGS

To those who have been called and gifted to specific works, you have the same appropriate response. Simply obey. If you haven't caught the drift yet, the overarching theme of this book seems to be obedience. No matter the arena in which you serve, obedience is always the key.

If the Spirit of God is directing you towards working in a cafe, teaching the Word full-time, or maybe living as a missionary overseas, your obedience will look different from others' as it plays out.

For example, the need to know and have confidence in every word of the scriptures remains the same, but your capacity for language may need to be a focus. Your understanding of cultural elements will need to be thought through. Can you live in a place where women do not have the same rights as men? Can you submit to the local laws and governance without bitterness for the sake of living and declaring the Gospel among those to whom you've been called?

In every situation where we see God call people into specific ministry, it is for His Glory. It is not that God prefers one of His servants over another as some are in the habit of thinking. God doesn't call some of us to a more "holy" ministry because of our capacity to understand Him or because we've earned it by being diligent in our morning study.

A side thought for your contemplation: perhaps the one

who is specifically diligent in setting apart time to spend in the Word hears His voice more clearly. Maybe because they are consuming the literal words of God daily and seeking His insights, they are just more likely to hear His call when He speaks to them.

Point being, God calls us all. Some of us may have a more specific task or a role that He has equipped us especially for. Maybe it is something you have a heart and passion for. On the contrary, maybe you are feeling called to someplace or somebody you have zero heart for. You don't even want to go. There are a few stories like that in the Bible, too. Remember Jonah? He literally wished the destruction of those God had called him to go to.

Be assured: God's purposes are fulfilled and His will is ultimately completed. Always. We can choose to be a joyful participant in the work or resist it. Imagine the joy we miss out on when we resist God's call and will.

Disobedience is a willful subjection to an agony that we should want no part of.

BIBLICAL EXAMPLES OF SPECIFIC CALLINGS

To look at an example from scripture of a specific calling to mission, let's see how God broke Nehemiah's heart for his people, and how that took shape as he obeyed.

The specific call of God on Nehemiah becomes evident as he hears about the need of his people and of the broken state of the gates in Jerusalem. In Nehemiah 1:2, he inquires into the state of the Jews who had escaped their exile and of the condition of their city. He is met with the knowledge of the broken walls and of the troubles his people were facing. We see the evidence in verse four that his heart immediately broke at this news.

Take note that it was through the course of Nehemiah's fasting and prayer that we see him move into a desire to do something in response. It does not appear at this point that he has the knowledge of what he could do, but he is fully aware of the need, and we see his heart bent towards a response. If you have a heart that is breaking for a place or people group, begin to fast and pray. The Lord will shape your heart and begin to develop your appropriate response.

Through his prayers, we see him ask God to bend His ear towards the plea, and Nehemiah repents not only for his sins, but also the sins of the nation. Then he finally implores God to remember His promises, and asks for mercy as he stands before the King. Here we see his calling begin to form, and then be confirmed as the Lord works within his heart.

A notable element in this story is that Nehemiah ended the first chapter by stating what it was he did as a profession. He worked in the king's court as a cup-bearer, so he clearly had an elevated platform from which to make his plea of the king. He was making use of what he had, and where he currently was. When he made his request of the king, he already had a plan detailed out. He was ready to do something, even though he did not yet have the resources.

When Nehemiah was finally given the chance to ask of the king and share his burden, he made very specific requests, above and beyond simply asking for time off from work.

The king saw Nehemiah's compassion for his people and gave him permission to go rebuild the gates. We see in 2:8 that, "*The king granted my requests, for the gracious hand of my God was on me.*" Here we see the call of God on Nehemiah confirmed through the blessing of the king and through provision for the task.

When God calls us, He will not only make a way to go but He will also make available what is required to complete the mission. This is a Biblical example of how God uses a situation and a burden to call someone into a specific task or environment.

In Acts 13:1-3, we see another example of the Lord calling others into His specific purposes through the working of the Holy Spirit and the local church body. It was in a time of worshipping and fasting that the Holy Spirit clearly spoke to the body and said, "*Set apart for me Barnabas and Saul...*"

The church quickly recognized God's voice and responded. They became partners in prayer and fasting for an extended time before sending those God had called out on mission. Prayer and fasting is a repeated theme when it comes to hearing the call of God in one's life. This should still be our response today when we begin to feel either a burden or a calling. Also, observe that it was a part of the New Testament Church's role to both recognize and affirm that calling.

If you are not actively involved in a local body but feel called to go on mission someplace specific, I would encourage you to find a gathering of believers to be the Church with you, to help grow you into spiritual maturity and to send you out when the time is appropriate.

Knowing and having confidence in your sending authority is again something to take note of here. Much like Nehemiah went with clear passage and provision because he was given the name and authority of King Artaxerxes, we have knowledge that our way is made clear by God.

We know that our provision and our power comes from the name of Jesus and the working of the Holy Spirit as we walk out our calling.

Being overwhelmingly sure of the one who sent us and the mission to which we are called, ensures that we can go for the period of time required. Having that surety will let us walk confidently through the trial and frustration that most certainly lies ahead, navigating it with a much greater perspective. Clarity will enable us to persevere until the work is finished.

AM I CALLED TO GO OR TO STAY?

I'm sorry, I cannot affirm that for you. Only you can truly determine this answer. If God is breaking your heart for a specific place or a people, and you indeed have the capacity to go, then the odds are high: you are called.

These are steps you can begin taking today to discern if you are to go overseas. Or if you are called to stay in your city. Or if you are called to start a gathering of the Church in your home. Or perhaps you are called to hold a steady job and proclaim the truth of the Gospel to your friends.

No matter what it is you are called to do, you should start doing these things:

- Read the Word.
- Gather as the Church.
- Get wise council.
- Pray more than you already do.
- Fast.
- Seek God relentlessly.

If you are to give financially to a mission or support it in another way, the Lord will reveal that to you. If you are called to go and do mission, trust the Lord will indeed reveal that to you as well. If you are truly a part of a Bible-teaching church with leaders who are also seeking God, then He will likely affirm it again through the spiritual leadership you submit to.

Not one single person can tell you if you are called to go. But I promise you, the Holy Spirit sure can. And He will, if you are asking and submitting.

Upon knowing if you are called to go or to stay: obey.

DEVELOPING A
HEART LIKE JESUS

To understand the heart of Jesus is to understand grace and mercy at a level few of us can comprehend. I am not graceful. I, in my selfishness, tend to look out for myself and expect grace to be given to me. But I normally don't show the level of grace that Jesus does.

To see how He does this, let's look at this story from John, where Jesus shows inexplicable grace to someone caught in their sin.

> *Then the scribes and the Pharisees brought a woman caught in adultery, making her stand in the center. "Teacher," they said to him, "this woman was caught in the act of committing adultery. In the law Moses commanded us to stone such women. So what do you say?" They asked this to trap him, in order that they might have evidence to accuse him. Jesus stooped down and started writing on the ground with his finger. When they persisted in questioning him, he stood up and said to them, "The one without sin among you should be the first to throw a stone at her." Then he stooped down again and continued writing on the ground. When they heard this, they left one by one, starting with the older men. Only he was left, with the woman in the center. When Jesus stood up, he said to her, "Woman, where are they? Has no one condemned you?" "No one, Lord," she answered. "Neither do I condemn you," said Jesus. "Go, and from now on do not sin anymore."*
> John 8:3-11

This story reveals God's heart in so many ways. It also reveals my heart, except I'm not the one who is loving and full of grace. I'm more closely found as one of those standing around with a rock in hand, judging and casting my opinion into the conversation.

Early on in our touring years, we had stopped in a dirty

suburb of Los Angeles to stay with friends for a night. I had gone alone to shop at a big box store nearby for something we needed.

As I walked into the store, my level of frustration rose. I was becoming so annoyed by the types of people I was encountering. They all looked like a product of their neighborhood. I remember specifically being frustrated at the way people acted, dressed, and treated both myself and others. I was literally angry at these people.

They had done no sin in that moment aside from being in my way and fitting every stereotype I had in my head. I was judging them to the very core, and I didn't even know their names.

Suddenly, as quickly as I had become bitter, I remember being fiercely convicted of my sin. As clear as could be, I felt the Spirit convict me of that judgmental attitude. My sin was laid bare before me, standing in the aisle. I knew what Jesus' heart was for those people, and I remember stopping and repenting.

Having felt such strong conviction, I decided to spend the rest of my time in that store praying under my breath for every person I saw.

What happened in the next sixty seconds transformed the way I view people even to this day. As I prayed for each person briefly, my heart began to break for them. I went from frustrated and angry to literally having tears in my eyes.

In prayer for them, God changed my heart to be more like His. I moved from anger to love. In the process of praying, my perspective changed.

I tell you this story because I want you to know that my flesh leans towards being a Pharisee in the account of the woman caught in adultery. I promise you, this is not a "look at how holy I am because I prayed for people" story. This is a story to highlight my extreme judgment of others. It was a moment of sinful nature confronted by the Holy Spirit.

When my friends (especially those who I think should know better) sin, it's so easy for me to discuss the failure with others and talk about how bad a choice they have made. It is easy for me to focus on their failure rather than on God's restitution.

The woman in the story from John was caught in the act of committing adultery. She was found guilty. But Jesus uses that moment to point out that all have sinned and fallen short of the glory of God (Romans 3:23). And then **He forgave her.**

I'm no less of a sinner than any person I've ever encountered anywhere on earth. Christ died for all of us. The quicker I can get to the point where I recognize my sin as the same as those around me, I can recognize that His grace is sufficient for all of us.

Something to consider is that this is equally as important in our Christian communities as it is in our relationship with those who are lost. Dietrich Bonhoeffer says in his book, *Life*

Together, "A Christian fellowship lives and exists by the intercession of its members for one another, or it collapses. I can no longer condemn or hate a brother for whom I pray, no matter how much trouble he causes me."

How can we pray with this perspective?

IMITATING JESUS

How is it that we can get to the point in which we imitate Christ in every situation without having to think it through? Can we get to the point in which our decisions are made through the lens of the Gospel instinctively? I believe we can. If we could not, then why would Paul have told us over and over again to strive to attain spiritual maturity? Paul's instructions lead us to believe that it is something we can achieve over the years of our Christian life.

A person is living a spiritually mature lifestyle when every decision they face and every action they take are filtered through the lens of the Word of God.

So how do we get there?

> *I am the true vine, and my Father is the gardener. Every branch in me that does not produce fruit he removes, and he prunes every branch that produces fruit so that*

> *it will produce more fruit. You are already clean because of the word I have spoken to you. Remain in me, and I in you. Just as a branch is unable to produce fruit by itself unless it remains on the vine, neither can you unless you remain in me.*
> John 15:1-4

The answer is simple. Remain in Christ.

If we stay in Him and are continually being pruned by the Spirit and the Word, then we will begin to live this way. We've already been made clean it says, because of His words. He has forgiven us our sins and restored us.

By staying **in** Him, we will continue to be refined and grow the fruit He desires us to grow. When I stay intentionally in the Word of God in the mornings, my attitude throughout the day is much more reflective of Him.

When I either forget or actively choose to abstain from the daily renewing of my mind (Romans 12:2), I can tell. My attitude is not like that of Christ. My thoughts about others are not like that of Christ. And suddenly, my actions and reactions toward others begin to reflect that.

We cannot bear the fruit we hope to bear without being attached to the vine. The believer aiming to imitate Christ will remain attached. Good fruit is produced by trees which are healthy in places that you cannot see.

> *My Father is glorified by this: that you produce much fruit and prove to be my disciples.*
> John 15:8

Jesus makes it clear that disciples are people who bear fruit. Remember, it is Him that bears the fruit in us, which then glorifies God. It is not our own striving to produce various fruits and works that reflect on Him.

FORGIVING LIKE JESUS DID

There are a thousand things to imitate that we could talk about in this book, but I think you will discover them for yourselves in greater depth if you spend more time in the Word. We should truly spend a lifetime examining the life of Jesus we ought to be copying. Here though, I will look at one in particular that I know impedes many believers from being fully engaged disciples. Forgiveness. **Forgiveness is not an option for the disciple of Jesus. It is a mandate.**

I believe that a lot of people will never experience the joy that God has for them because of their unwillingness to forgive. It holds them back from the freedom that God intends.

Our example of forgiveness comes from the cross. Not only was Jesus paying the price, but God was actively forgiving the sins of the world through it.

Realize this: Jesus was verbalizing forgiveness along with His agonizing screams, at the moment the nails were being driven through His wrists. As He was being pinned to the cross, what words do we see Him express in the midst of the excruciating pain?

Luke 23:34 shows us the very words He spoke: "*Father, forgive them, for they do not know what they do.*" **In the very moment He was being wronged, He was forgiving them.**

I would assert that any moment past the offense in which we carry un-forgiveness in our heart is a moment we are walking in sin. Someone imitating Christ will forgive, and forgive quickly.

I've heard many people (believers included) say things like, "I will forgive them, I just need a moment to process it." This is the absolute wrong response for a person aiming to be a disciple imparting the hope of the Gospel in the world.

Trust me, this challenges me too. Forgiving those who wrong us is one of the hardest things to put into practice daily, but it is the easiest way to show who Jesus is.

If your neighbor, co-worker, or family member has offended or wronged you, make it a point to tell them you've forgiven them, even if they haven't asked for it. And, you are sorry for any bitterness or sin in your response which was caused by the situation.

The likely response from them will be confusion or a loss for words. They might even ask, "Why now, after all these years?" And there you have it. You now hold the perfect moment in which to share the Gospel with them.

"Well, Christ has forgiven me of my failures," you might say, "and I am now able to love you because of the love He has for me."

Think about this: you have basically just explained the Gospel to them. God is love, I'm a sinner, love covers sin, and now our relationship is repaired.

You may or may not have the opportunity for more conversation after that. But I assure you, that person will walk away knowing and remembering that you forgave them because Christ forgave you, regardless of who wronged who.

Before you continue reading, I would urge you to examine your heart and ask the Lord to reveal to you anyone you need to forgive. Maybe a phone call or a meeting is in order at this very moment.

> *If possible, as far as it depends on you, live at peace with everyone.*
> Romans 12:18

Part Two: Preparing

SHIFTING OUR FOCUS

Proper preparation to live on mission requires immense sacrifice. I'm continually challenged in my own life by how many things I still need to put down in order to be living in reflection of Jesus.

At the time that I am writing this, I have spent more than fifteen years of my life as a touring musician, traveling for long distances in small vehicles with a lot of different personalities and people. Nothing has challenged my flesh and revealed how much of a sinner I am more than this experience. I'm so grateful for the time I've spent on the road, learning with and from others how to put my preferences aside.

It becomes clearer every day that my personal preference

matters more to me than other people's comfort. Being in a band is a lot like having four roommates in a fifty square-foot flat. No space is your own. No moment is private.

In order for our band to not break up over the years, we really had to put into practice what Paul talks about in Colossians 3. I won't put the entire scripture right here, but I challenge you to pause and go read it now.

I want to look at how he tells the church to live in this chapter. We will break it into three specific actions we must take in order to live peaceably and reflect Christ.

FOCUS ON ETERNAL THINGS

"So if you have been raised with Christ, seek the things above..."

Colossians 3:1

In order for us to survive the van, we had to align our focus correctly. When we focused on the eternal reasons for our pursuits, small things stopped mattering. **When you look at the long view, you can put aside personal preference because you begin to realize those things matter so little in light of eternity.**

Paul tells them that if you are a new creation in Christ, stop looking at the small things. Set your focus on things that truly bear weight into eternity!

Shifting your focus is not something you do on accident, but rather it becomes truly possible when you are in Christ and are being renewed daily by the transforming of your mind.

I referenced Romans 12:2 a while ago, and I do it again here because it is another vital piece of our Christian life. Our minds get renewed so that we **can** focus on eternal things when we are immersed in the Word of God and letting it do Its work in us.

> *Therefore, brothers and sisters, in view of the mercies of God, I urge you to present your bodies as a living sacrifice, holy and pleasing to God; this is your true worship. Do not be conformed to this age, but be transformed by the renewing of your mind, so that you may discern what is the good, pleasing, and perfect will of God.*
> *Romans 12:1-2*

Part Two: Preparing

PUT OFF THESE THINGS

"Therefore, put to death what belongs to your earthly nature: sexual immorality, impurity, lust, evil desire, and greed, which is idolatry. Because of these, God's wrath is coming upon the disobedient, and you once walked in these things when you were living in them."

Colossians 3:5-7

Paul tells the church to put off all of these things: sexual immorality, wrong passions, evil desires, and idolatry. He tells them to stop living in these ways because they do not reflect a life that is being renewed daily and transformed by the Word. Jesus died for these sins, so we are to stop living in them.

Romans 6:1 says *"What should we say then? Should we continue in sin so that grace may multiply?"*

By no means! Grace indeed covers our failures, but our new nature should long to please God. **We stop sinning because we begin to separate from the attributes of the flesh that look like us in our humanity, and put on those which reflect Christ in His divinity.**

PUT ON THESE THINGS

"Therefore, as God's chosen ones, holy and dearly loved, put on compassion, kindness, humility, gentleness, and patience, bearing with one another and forgiving one another if anyone has a grievance against another. Just as the Lord has forgiven you, so you are also to forgive. Above all, put on love, which is the perfect bond of unity. And let the peace of Christ, to which you were also called in one body, rule your hearts. And be thankful. Let the word of Christ dwell richly among you, in all wisdom teaching and admonishing one another through psalms, hymns, and spiritual songs, singing to God with gratitude in your hearts. And whatever you do, in word or in deed, do everything in the name of the Lord Jesus, giving thanks to God the Father through him."

Colossians 3:12-17

There is a lot in this piece of text to take in, but right away we are told we need to "put on" certain attributes. Each one of these attributes concerns the way we interact with other people: tender mercies, kindness, humility, gentleness, patience.

Personally, if I were to put those on for the sake of my marriage, our relationship would be transformed. Applying these natures to any interpersonal relationship will instantly change it for the better.

In the context of the body of Christ, what would happen if we began to employ these things? The Church would be transformed! What if our churches started to forgive any and all complaints we have about one another?

I have traveled to a lot of different churches throughout my life. And if there is one thing churches do well, it is talk or complain about what other churches in their town are doing.

For the sake of the Gospel, stop this immediately! For the sake of the lost in our communities, put on tender mercies in the way that we deal with one another. Put on love! It is the bond of perfection and the evidence of our salvation. This statement in itself should be enough for us. I want to be held in that bond.

I know I am held sure by the love of Christ, found in His Kingdom and in the mercies He has shown me. But that begs the question in response; am I finding and regarding others in that same way?

If we are to be well-equipped for the mission, we need to learn to focus on eternal things, put off our sinful natures, and put on the likeness of Christ. Only then will we be able to effectively engage in the mission that we have been called into.

THE SPIRIT EQUIPS US

Praise God that it is not up to me and my efforts to accomplish these things Paul has told us to do. I struggle to put off sin. It takes everything in me to bear with others in love. I'm so glad to know that we have the Holy Spirit working in and through us to help us accomplish these things.

You would be wise not to try to do this in your own power. You will fall short every time. **We were given this Helper from God to help us endure.**

It is important that we know the job of and rely on the power of the Spirit of God to live on mission.

HE CONVICTS US

"Every conviction must be carried out into action. Christ's commands were meant to be obeyed."

– Andrew Murray

There are a great many roles of the Holy Spirit in our lives, but one of them that is worthy of our attention as we prepare to go on mission is the way He convicts us of sin.

Far too many people mistake the conviction of the Holy Spirit for the guilt and shame of condemnation. In fact, it is something we ought to celebrate! It is because God loves us with an unrelenting love that He gave us the Holy Spirit to do the work of bringing us back into healthy communion with Himself.

When a Christ follower is in sin, the Holy Spirit is hard at work bringing to their minds the truth of the Word and pulling them into repentance.

In John 16, Jesus describes for us the roles of the Holy Spirit. It says that He is the one who convicts the world.

Conviction should not be feared by the believer, but rather celebrated.

Because of His undying love for us, God sent a way back to Himself for when we depart from the unity He desires. Sin separates us from God, but through Jesus we have unity restored. The Spirit continues to strengthen that unified relationship by ensuring we can hear and know the truth from God.

Jesus tells us:

> *When the Spirit of truth comes, he will guide you into all the truth. For he will not speak on his own, but he will speak whatever he hears. He will also declare to you what is to come. He will glorify me, because he will take from what is mine and declare it to you. Everything the Father has is mine. This is why I told you that he takes from what is mine and will declare it to you.*
> John 16:13-14

Learn to listen to the nudge of the Holy Spirit in your life. It will bear you much joy as you obey His direction and call you into perfect unity with the Father. We should have such security in knowing that we can hear Him speak to us. If you struggle with insecurity, you should know that is not God's desire for you. You can walk in confidence as a Christian, knowing that God desires to speak to you and give you the authority you lack.

As people living on mission, we need to be actively listening to His voice as He guides us throughout the day.

So the next logical question becomes: how do we hear it?

Part Two: Preparing

RECOGNIZING THE VOICE OF THE HOLY SPIRIT

If we are followers of Jesus, we will be able to recognize His voice. As He speaks to us through the Holy Spirit, we will begin to recognize the sound and nature of His voice to us as we walk with Him.

We are given the assurance by Jesus Himself that we will be able to recognize when He speaks. He teaches the disciples in John 10:4 that even though others may come and try to lead the sheep off, they will recognize His voice.

There may be times that people being led astray will choose to ignore the fact that something is off with what they are being taught or told. We ought to guard our hearts and allow the promises and truths of the Word to be so ingrained into our understanding that we can resist the temptations and enticements of any voice other than our Father.

Jesus says that He is the Good Shepherd. No one can snatch us from the Father's hand when we have come to the Father through Him.

If we will come to know His voice, how then can we sense the prompting of it? One of the most common questions I've heard among believers and non-believers alike is, "How do I distinguish between my own thoughts and His?"

I believe there is a time-tested answer to this, and it may seem almost too simple: be in the Word.

There will be times the voice of the Spirit may come in our thoughts, which can often be difficult to discern. We will examine how to do this in a moment. What we do know without hesitation, though, is that His voice is always going to be heard when we open the Word of God and read it.

When we put the assurances and the steadfast promises written in the Word into our heart, we begin to know with extreme clarity the thoughts and intents of God.

His voice is astoundingly clear and hard to misinterpret when we read it in textual form.

When we study the written Word, we start to clearly see the mannerisms and character of God exemplified, showing us how to recognize His commands when He gives them. If, for example, I am walking by a homeless person on the street and I feel the urge to give them the money in my wallet, I can weigh that urge against what I know of God through the Word.

I know for certain that is not my flesh speaking, because outside of the transformed person I am in Christ, I would never want to give them my money! My fleshly nature is to say, "get a job," or to ignore them altogether and just walk on by.

But, if I sense the urge or have a thought that I should give that person my money, and I then weigh this thought against the truth I know of God from His Word, then it may be the voice of the Spirit prompting me.

I know God's nature and character is generous. I know

this for sure because He sent Jesus, His own son. There could be no more generous gift He could give.

I also know His heart is for the poor.

I also know His heart is for the least of these.

So it turns out, I already know His character when I know the Word.

When I weigh those thoughts against the truths and natures of God versus my own, I know that it is not my own thought that I am having. Instead, it is one guided by the Spirit of God to show that person love and engage with them.

Consider this: to know and recognize His voice is similar to the way that I might recognize the voice of my own wife. If you called me on the phone, I would likely have to ask who it is, since I may not have heard your voice with any frequency.

But if my wife calls me, and only sneezed on the phone, I would know it was her instantly. Why? Because of the depth of relationship I have developed with her over the years of time together.

Time together gives you a keen ability to recognize one's voice. Time in the Word of God will give you the ability to recognize the voice of God when He speaks to you.

THE NECESSITY OF BEING SPIRITUALLY MATURE

I have referenced spiritual maturity a lot in these pages, for both those preparing to go on mission overseas and those living out their walk with Jesus at home. There truly is great need that we grow in maturity. It is God's desire for us to mature, and it should be our earnest desire as well.

I love observing that the greater the depth of Paul's spiritual maturity, the more he recognized the depravity of his flesh and the depth of his own sin. The longer he lived with the Holy Spirit, the greater sinner he claimed to be.

Growth in spiritual maturity helps you to identify your

sinful natures and leads you to repent of them and continue the process of sanctification that God intends.

Thankfully and ashamedly, every day that I live I realize more and more how great of a sinner I am. In turn, every day I confess my sin and come to Jesus, the greater understanding I have of His love and grace.

> *We have a great deal to say about this, and it is difficult to explain, since you have become too lazy to understand. Although by this time you ought to be teachers, you need someone to teach you the basic principles of God's revelation again. You need milk, not solid food. Now everyone who lives on milk is inexperienced with the message about righteousness, because he is an infant. But solid food is for the mature—for those whose senses have been trained to distinguish between good and evil.*
> *Hebrews 5:11-14*

We need to grow past the need for simple milk and begin consuming solid food, which is for the mature! This is entirely possible through training and the guidance of the Spirit.

Scripture commands that we stop being immature.

WHERE DO WE LOOK?

I've been a believer for a long time, most of my memorable life, honestly. I could tell you story after story of seeing God provide for my needs in astounding ways. I've seen the miraculous occur in people's lives as they have been healed in an instant.

And yet it never fails; when I face my next insurmountable problem, I forget to look to Jesus. It seems like every day I encouter something that I should take to Him, instead I get to work on my own, hoping to produce some sort of miracle in my own power.

If I am growing in spiritual maturity, I will stop looking to my own capacity first. Spiritually mature people look to Jesus first.

Personally I'm encouraged when I read the Bible because I see that the disciples did this all the time. Literally, they were walking with Jesus every day and they seemed to fall apart at the sight of impending trouble.

Earlier I referenced the story of when Jesus fed the five thousand men, and then just a short while later He fed four thousand more. When I look at how the disciples forgot who they were with and who solved the problem last time, I see my own failures wrapped up in their words and disbelief.

What reveals their lack of maturity is where they looked first. They looked at the problem, both times.

Part Two: Preparing

> *So when Jesus looked up and noticed a huge crowd coming toward him, he asked Philip, "Where will we buy bread so that these people can eat?" He asked this to test him, for he himself knew what he was going to do.*
> *John 6:5-6*

Jesus was testing Philip. Obviously he failed. Jesus already had the solution!

He knew that Philip had just seen the distribution of the bread at the last miracle. I imagine He hoped Philip would respond with, "What are you looking at me for? You're God!" But he didn't.

The problem was not that Philip didn't believe that Jesus could solve the problem. **The issue is, like us, Philip looked at the problem in front of him, not the solution standing next to him.**

Jesus will often position us to watch Him work and involve us in the process. In these times, we have such an incredible opportunity to grow in our maturity and in our perspective. Think of this astounding thought with the Great Commission in mind. Jesus literally has invited us to participate in the redemption of the created being with its Creator!

As Jesus lived with and led His disciples, He was teaching them to constantly look at **Him** instead of at their problem. If you can learn that lesson, you will be walking in a depth of maturity that few believers ever get to.

I believe there is a difference between being a Christian and being a spiritually mature Christian. The difference is that spiritually mature Christians look to Jesus over and over again.

Spiritual maturity produces spiritual perspective.

When I look at my daily problems with my finite, human perspective, they look insurmountable. When I step back for a wider view and realize that the solution is Jesus, those same problems look miniscule. We must learn to view the impossible from further away and realize that God already knows how He intends to solve it.

Our role as a believer maturing in Christ is to trust Him. He is trustworthy.

HOW DO WE ACT?

If I am becoming a mature Christian, I am responsible for a Christlike response. Philippians 2:14-15 says to, "Do *everything without grumbling and arguing, so that you may be blameless and pure, children of God who are faultless in a crooked and perverted generation, among whom you shine like stars in the world.*"

If we are Christians, then walking out our daily life requires making some hard choices and decisions.

The true test of making hard choices comes when I am

faced with doing something I don't personally want to do. Can I do this thing without grumbling or complaining?

This is challenging enough without ever leaving the church walls! If I'm being honest, it is difficult without even leaving the tiny group of believers that I'm associated with daily. Complaining to each other is so easy to do. We call it a lot of different things: venting, getting it off our chest, talking it through, etc. The list goes on.

Let's call it what it is, Church. We complain a lot.

How can we look at this command to put aside our grumbling and expect anything other than a confrontation with our sinful selves? How can we claim to be heading into our communities and into the world on mission if we can't even stop complaining about the sound of the worship team?

How can we expect to act as mature people, shining as lights in a perverse generation, when we can't subject our own preferences to be diminished for the sake of another in the body?

Our example lies again in the person of Jesus Christ. He, who is Lord over all, was subjected to the agony of the cross.

Earlier in the chapter, Paul tell us:

> *Adopt the same attitude as that of Christ Jesus, who, existing in the form of God, did not consider equality with God as something to be exploited. Instead he emptied himself by assuming the form of a servant, taking*

> *on the likeness of humanity. And when he had come as a man, he humbled himself by becoming obedient to the point of death—even to death on a cross.*
> *Philippians 2:5-8*

If we cannot make it through a church service without complaining, how are we acting as Christ? He made Himself as lowly as He could possibly be, for the sake of the very people who beat Him and crucified Him. There is no greater depth of humility than what He did for us. **How dare we grumble and complain over temporal things.**

Paul continues and says when we stop grumbling and complaining, that's when we can become blameless and pure children of God. If we are now found in Christ and have been given this new identity as a child of God, our actions should reflect this.

When a new prince or princess is brought into a royal family, they are trained in the ways in which to act. They are expected to dress as royalty, dine in the appropriate manner, and change their lifestyle to match that of their new royal family.

Oughtn't we change our mannerisms to reflect the new identity which we have been given through the cross? Should not we live in a manner that reflects Christ? Are we not commanded to do so?

Take note: it is not our works that make us blameless, but

the work of Christ. Our identity and life is changed as we are born into this new family.

By doing these things, Paul says we will shine as lights in the midst of a perverse generation. There is no greater way for us to share the Gospel audibly than to live lives that demand question. Live your life in such a way that others will ask why you're different.

Why do we live this way? Because we are children of God.

When we learn to prefer others above ourselves and to stop grumbling and complaining, then we will be able to live lives that look different from most of our community.

Look at Ephesians 4. Paul is imploring the believers to act in unity. He literally says in verse one to walk, "*worthy of the calling you have received...*" These are such strong words to the Church. What a heavy weight of responsibility. Consider that when we are told to walk worthy, a part of that burden is on us to carry. We are actually responsible to walk out our lives in an appropriate manner.

His exact words tell us we should be, "*with all humility and gentleness, with patience, bearing with one another in love, making every effort to keep the unity of the Spirit through the bond of peace*" (Ephesians 4:2-3).

In Romans 12:18 he says, "*as far as it depends on you, live at peace with everyone.*"

Our every effort should be to live peaceably with others, in all the situations we encounter through our day. When we do this, we affirm the reality of God in our lives by our actions. Our ability to live in peace with those around us is evidence that God is alive and that He has transformed us. **Though they claim to long for peace, humanity resists living in peace. It is the exact opposite of our nature to live in peace, because sin is always at war within us.**

There will never be peace on earth until the return of Jesus. For those of us with eternal perspective, we understand that this is a feeble and meaningless pursuit. Only in Jesus is their peace. Exemplify that today, and make every effort to live at peace with others for the sake of the Gospel.

Spiritually mature people act like Jesus and live in unity.

WHAT DO WE SAY?

Spiritually mature people say less. If you want to read scripture that backs up this statement, go read the book of Proverbs. All of it.

Any person who has played the word game Scrabble knows that the power of a well-placed word can change the game.

The Bible addresses the way we use our words over, and over, and over again. God knew that those to whom He had given free will would make regular abuse of the freedoms He gave to express themselves. From the time we learn to speak, we are learning how to use our words to accomplish our own purposes. Even small children learn what words get them attention or food and begin to use them in their vocabulary.

The impact of well-timed words will do one of two very different things. Depending on our use of them, they can either inflict maximum damage on another person or encourage them into life.

> *Death and life are in the power of the tongue, and those who love it will eat its fruit.*
> *Proverbs 18:21*

Throughout the entirety of the Word, we see how it teaches us to refrain from our tendencies and speak things that matter. Proverbs 18:2 says: "A *fool does not delight in understanding, but only wants to show off his opinions."*

We live in a modern era in which every tool imaginable is given us to express our opinion to the world. But in the age of sharing our thoughts instantly, we may actually be able to say more when we say less. When we do not feel that we have to express our opinion on every matter, political and personal, we will be a much greater voice for the Gospel.

Here is a basic thesis on this statement:

The more of our personal opinion we express, the more likely we are to distance those around us who may disagree. By expressing strong opinions on things that do not bear weight into eternity, we limit our opportunity to speak to the things of actual eternal importance. **Stop impeding your chances of sharing Jesus by speaking your mind on topics that don't matter.**

The longer I live, the more I realize that what I have to say matters very little. My thoughts and opinions bear very little weight on eternity unless I'm speaking the truth given to us by God. The more spiritually mature we become, the less we feel the need to express our opinion.

TAKE IT SLOW

> *My dear brothers and sisters, understand this: Everyone should be quick to listen, slow to speak, and slow to anger, for human anger does not accomplish God's righteousness.*
> *James 1:19-20*

How you respond to things in everyday life matters. All throughout scripture we are told to refrain from speaking, except on matters concerning good doctrine and the hope of the Gospel. Of those things, we are actually commanded to speak up! This means that everything we say, filtered through a Gospel lens, should be pointing those around us and the rest of the world to the only hope we truly have: Jesus.

Society ebs and flows. Talking points change.

The Church is indeed commanded to be a part of the world, engaged in reform when beneficial and speaking up for those in harm's way.

But what we say matters in these moments. We should point to the eternal hope we have, rather than the temporary solutions we can offer.

We are faced with an interesting contrast: we are to use our voice in the world speaking the hope of Jesus, yet also told to stop talking about pretty much everything else.

Slow your responses and let them be Gospel driven.

Proverbs 17:28 says that even a fool is thought wise when he doesn't speak! The thing is that what we say reveals our heart and who we are. When we speak quickly and out of emotional response, it most commonly reveals our impatience. **When we refrain our words and choose to speak in a mature way, it reveals how the Gospel has changed you.**

Once your words leave your mouth, there is no recanting them. Ask any person running for political office about how hard it is to retract words spoken too quickly. At times, a spiritually-mature person can effectively say more when they actually say less. This is a hard thing to put into practice, though, because every bit of our flesh wants to express ourselves through our words.

It is always easy to say something, and then even harder to take it back. For example, in matters of commitments, we love to make promises and assure others what we can (or think we can) do. How many people have I personally disappointed by overcommitting myself with my words when I knew full well it would be difficult to deliver?

My point is simple: if we want to reflect the Gospel more clearly and be obedient to the Great Commission, we will speak often and with boldness, but it will be less about what we think and more about what we know of Jesus.

Spiritually mature people use words wisely.

Part Two: Preparing

THE ROLE OF A HEALTHY CHURCH COMMUNITY

If you are called to and preparing for living on mission in a place that takes you from your home and your local community, then you should carefully examine the way that the missionaries were sent out from the early Church.

Barnabas and Saul were sent out of the church at Antioch in Acts 13. The role of the church is in part outlined here. I want us to see a few things that the local church was involved in during the process.

In verse two we see "As *they were worshiping the Lord and fasting*," the Holy Spirit spoke. Take note, you who are called, your ministry does not start when you arrive on the field.

Those whom the Lord called in this chapter were actively involved in the ministry to the Lord in the place they were already. The Lord will call and equip us, yes, but don't wait for the calling to go to a foreign place before you begin to be a part of the ministry happening in your town.

We will discuss prayer and fasting next, but note that in the first few verses of Acts 13, it mentions that they were fasting, twice. It was an active part of their communion with God.

In many of our churches today we have selectively decided what is important and what is not. Fasting seems to have fallen by the wayside.

When people throughout scripture were actively seeking God for something, they sacrificed their meals for the sake of the process of prayer and seeking deeper intimacy with the Almighty.

We have already observed that those who were sent by the church were actively involved in the local gathering of the church. How involved are you? Are you engaged in being the Church today alongside others? Are you withholding your involvement because of some preference, opinion, or disagreement?

If you are not actively engaged in being the Church at home, growing in community and relational health, how could you ever expect to build a healthy community of faith overseas?

I want us to really take a good look at this part: it was in their time of ministry, prayer, and fasting that they heard the voice of the Holy Spirit tell them to send Barnabas and Saul for the work to which He had called them.

They heard the voice of the Spirit speak to them, during their times of spiritual disciplines, **as they engaged** in the work of the Church. I love the example they set by their prompt return to even **more** prayer and fasting to confirm the command of God! The early Church remained in the disciplines in which they heard the voice of God speak. We need to apply this example immediately.

When we hear the voice of God call us into a work, we too quickly assume we know the how and the when, and just begin. If we are to walk in these callings fully and in the manner exemplified by the church at Antioch, we should be drenching the whole thing in prayer and fasting.

Seek God always, and obey the commands of Jesus to His Church. This is when the early disciples took action on their callings. The church laid hands on the disciples, prayed some more, and sent them away. The church sent them away, but the Spirit is the one who sent them **out**.

There is a difference in the two different uses of the word "sent." In verse three, the word used for "sent" comes from the Greek word meaning "to release." The church's job was not to call them, but to release them to do the work to which they were called.

The Greek translation for the word "sent out" in verse four would have been used to say they were sent away, or sent out.

The work of the Spirit is different from the work of the Church in this context. The Church releases the minister, the Spirit sends them on route.

We will discuss in greater depth the need for the believer to be fully engaged in a local church context wherever possible later on. I want us to completely understand that the believer needs to be engaged in the Body of Christ to be healthy. This is where the confirmation of calling can be identified, and the Christian can work out their faith alongside people, examining the Word while spending time being refined together.

We need to be a part of the Church to go on mission as the Church.

> *Whenever we minister together, it is easier for people to recognize that we do not come in our own name, but in the name of the Lord Jesus who sent us.*
> *— Henri Nouwen, In the Name of Jesus*

PRAYER

> *Prayer and the Word have one common center—God. Prayer seeks God; the Word reveals God. In prayer, man asks God; in the Word, God answers man.*
> *— Andrew Murray*

When we are a people who wrestle endlessly in prayer, we will be people marked by the presence of God.

Jesus wrestled in prayer regularly. The disciples were taught to be in prayer by Jesus. Paul tells the Thessalonians to pray without ceasing (1 Thessalonians 5:17).

If we miss this command, we miss one of the greatest

opportunities we have as a created being: to interact directly with our Creator. We have no limitations on our words when we engage in prayer. We can tell God our hearts' desires, we can tell Him of our brokenness and of our longing for comfort. We can bring all our needs before Him directly. We can enthrone Him above our problems through exaltation when we pray. We have the chance to give Him the glory, to shout His name in victory, and to worship Him for who He is.

Jesus gave us the example of how we can pray when He taught the disciples in Matthew 6 and Luke 11. He gave them a model of what a prayer should look like that both glorifies God and presents our requests and daily needs to Him. We should pray as Jesus instructed.

If you are a believer hoping to be more intentional in sharing the Gospel and living on mission, then you must be someone who believes in the power of prayer.

Through prayer, Jesus interceded on our behalf in John 17. He prayed that we may be one with the Father as He is. We have the Word speaking to us, and the Spirit speaking to us. So we also have the ability to speak to God through this simple discipline. I identify this as a discipline because it requires immense intentionality.

I'm not talking about moments of distress. Calling out to God in our weakest moments is easy. The discipline of prayer requires us to stop what we are doing in our daily lives and engage with God, even when we're not fully aware of the needs we might have. **The discipline of prayer moves it from needs-based to relationship-based.**

To miss the opportunity we have to be in direct communication with the Father is to miss one of the grand joys of our time on earth.

Jesus invites us to present our requests to God in prayer. In Matthew 7, and also in Luke 11, we read where Jesus says, "*Ask, and it will be given to you. Seek, and you will find. Knock, and the door will be opened to you.*"

God clearly knows our needs and understands them, but in the process of presenting our requests to God, we submit to that knowledge. By taking these things to God in prayer, we acknowledge His sovereignty and our need of Him. He loves hearing our prayers. He loves when we invite Him to work on our behalf. In all of these things He receives the glory!

When our temporal earthly needs are met by His mighty hand after we have submitted them to Him in prayer, we can gleefully celebrate His response when it comes.

Sometimes our prayers are not answered.

Sometimes we seek God for years on an issue or topic and seem to have no response. But God is working all of them together for our good and for His glory in His time.

Take the example of Joseph in the book of Genesis. His father lost his most cherished son when his brothers sold Joseph to be a slave. He was imprisoned unfairly, punished for crimes he never committed, and seemingly forsaken. I imag-

Part Two: Preparing

ine that Joseph regularly called out to God in agony of his loss, wondering why he, who loved God, was being forgotten and abandoned by Him.

In God's perfect timing, though, we know that Joseph was removed from prison and established as the ruler over the land. When a famine struck the land, the same brothers who had sold Joseph into slavery came to unknowingly seek his help.

Joseph had been placed in a position to enact revenge for the agony and pain his family had caused him. Instead, he sought the restoration of his family.

Joseph is an astoundingly close picture to the life of Jesus. Jesus was taken from his rightful place in the Godhead and put into the lowly position of being a human, only to be spat upon and beaten by those He loved, the very family He Himself had created. He was wrongfully crucified, but was then taken from the prison of death and brought back to life. In conquering death and the grave, He was able to pay the price for those of us who were perishing. The whole reason this occurred was to point us to Jesus, and to give us right perspective of who God is.

Jospeh was not actually abandoned. Although he felt he had been, and though every earthly evidence was stacked against him, God was working all things together for a good he could not see. What his own brothers intended as harm, God worked for their own good! The brother they delivered to slavery was able to deliver them in the time of famine.

Trust God, seek Him always, and remember Who it is that is working things out.

Getting ready to do mission requires having the mind of Christ, which comes when you intercede with Him through prayer and the Word.

Part Two: Preparing

FASTING

Fasting is a manner of denying oneself and his or her inner appetites. It is a denial of our human desire to invoke the working of God to be manifested in our lives.

Our bodies and flesh deeply desire to intake food and other pleasurable things.

To fast is to sacrifice our personal desire to see the revelation of God in our human, earthly environment.

Through fasting, we sacrifice the temporal to see the eternal revealed. We believe that God is sovereign and that He knows all things as they are and as they will be. We see it evidenced throughout scripture that God's mind was often changed through the work of fasting.

It could be stated that, though God's mind is already made up, through our fasting we invoke His mercy and involvement in our situation. In the Old Testament book of Jonah, we see that even though the city of Nineveh was condemned by God, it was spared as they fasted and prayed, asking for God's salvation despite their previous judgment. When Jonah preached repentance, they responded, which invoked a change of God's heart concerning their destruction.

It is not that God changed His mind entirely, because He sovereignly knew they would repent. Rather, He revoked His condemnation because of their repentance. Does that sound familiar? I'll give you a hint: this is the Gospel! In this manner we see that the act of fasting bears great weight in the change of their situation. Through fasting, prayer, and repentance, they revealed their desire to see God glorified as they submitted to Him.

God's mind is made up, but repentance and fasting shows the sovereign God that, through humility and sacrifice, you come pleading a cause. Fasting presents the heart of a humble servant requesting the involvement of a capable God.

To fast is to humble oneself and abstain from your own desires, while inviting God to involve Himself in your life or the lives of those around you in a powerful way. Fasting is an act of great submission, not to change the mind of an omniscient God, but to implore His mercy.

A fast done in the right heart is an act done in recognition of God's holiness. It is an understanding that the sovereign God is in control of all things. **We bring our needs before God, not because He is unaware of them but because we recognize His authority over them.**

Fasting pleads with God to reveal His mercy and His heart in a situation that we likely do not understand. It is a manner of setting ourselves apart for God so that we may understand His heart more clearly and implore His revelation to us.

A truly humble submission to His providence and provision aligns us with the will of God for His people. It is a chance to recognize that He is truly Lord over all.

To fast is to abstain from food or another thing as the Spirit leads. In our current day, we see many people abstain from technology or other various elements in the name of fasting. To our loss, we often view the Biblical version of fasting as antiquated and obsolete.

I would challenge you to delve into a deep study of the act of fasting. There are books like, *God's Chosen Fast* by Arthur Wallis, which address the topic at greater length and with much depth.

I believe that when we minimize the impact of a true fast in our lives by choosing to simply abstain from a few pleasures, such as technology or coffee, we lessen the intended impact of God's design for a fast. There is a difference in giving up something we want (like technology) to carve out more time **for** God than sacrificing something we **need** (food) to implore God of His mercy and seek His guidance.

This statement may push some buttons, but realize that throughout the Bible when people fasted, they actually fasted from food. People learning to live on mission should be applying Biblical principles the Biblical way.

Jesus taught us to fast, so we should probably fast.

JESUS FASTED

Jesus fasted for forty days and forty nights before He completed the work which He was sent to do (Matthew 4).

During this time, He was tempted by Satan with food. He was tempted with the opportunity to fulfill His earthly human desires by eating. He chose rather to reply with the Word of God. Let this be an example; when we are faced with a challenge from the enemy, we need to know the Word of God deeply. Jesus rebuked the temptation of the enemy by quoting the truth of the scriptures.

When we abstain from food for the sake of pleading before God, we are choosing to make our flesh subservient to our spiritual needs. By prioritizing time on our face before God over food, we are subjecting our bodies to a form of discipline.

Adam and Eve were caught by the enemy's deceit, falling prey to their physical hunger and longing for that which they could not have. The entire story of Jacob and Esau is based around man's hunger being elevated above the value of birthright.

Countless Christians today suffer from a struggle of appetite and food consumption. Like many other temporal things, food can often be a false comfort, replacing or distracting from the intended design of a spiritual comfort found only in the Gospel.

The enemy has been using food as a means of distraction from God's eternal purposes since the dawn of time. Is it any surprise to us that the abstention from food would be a spiritual discipline that can cause us to consecrate ourselves before God?

Go read Isaiah 58. It deals with the elevation of the act of fasting itself over the purposes of fasting. It also points to a time when God's people fasted and yet abused their workers, or cried out to God and yet carried on in their wickedness. If we are fasting just for fasting's sake, we are simply swelling up our own pride. That type of fast will do little to turn the heart of God towards our plea.

The Pharisees were excellent at this and had set apart multiple days of fasting each week. This was done as a work that supposedly made them holier than others. This did nothing but become a religious tradition which held no power.

To see results, our fasting must be done with the right heart. We must recognize God's power, humbly implore of

Him, and submit to His answers. God does not implement the task of fasting as a mandatory element of our spirituality, nor as something we do to achieve salvation. Rather, **God desires the act of fasting to be done with a heart of submission and supplication, revealing to God the depth of our desires to see Him involved in our situations.**

When any part of our spiritual life becomes a simple task we check off in our day, we risk the devaluation of its role in our life. To be obedient to the Word of God means that we will do all of these disciplines in such a way that we come before God broken and contrite, eager to see Him glorified through our actions.

HIS DISCIPLES FASTED

In Acts 13, we see the disciples fast, pray, and worship regularly. When Saul and Barnabas were set apart for the ministry, the church joined together to fast and seek the Spirit's guidance before sending them out. The putting off of physical nourishment was a choice they made in order to seek the Spirit's involvement in their decision.

Fasting is not solely a work to be done by oneself, but rather can be done as a body. Throughout scripture, we see groups of people called to fast together to implore God's engagement in their situation.

To fast is to obey the scripture. To obey the invitation and command of God is to sacrifice personal desire for the sake of intentional supplication. Supplication is the act of presenting your requests before God. It means pleading humbly before God for a particular cause, need, or desire.

What might happen if we took up this practice of the scriptures? What would change if we became a people so distraught over the state of both our sins and our nation's sins that we sought God's involvement with regularity? If the Church would come before God with earnest fasting and supplication, how would our world begin to change?

Why have we given up these theologically sound instructions and lessened them to the point of simply sacrificing our technology for a day?

Healthy disciples and people preparing to live out the mission of Christ will submit all of their desires and longings to the Spirit. Modern disciples will be willing to engage in times of fasting and prayer as they long for God to reveal Himself and be glorified in their lives, their families, and their cities.

Part Three: Becoming

PART THREE.

BECOMING PEOPLE WHO WILL CHANGE THE WORLD

LIVING ON PURPOSE

> *True Christianity aims at having the character of Christ so formed in us, that in our most ordinary activities His temperament and attitudes reveal themselves. The Spirit and the will of Christ should so possess us that in our relationships with people, in our leisure time, and in our daily business it will be second nature for us to act like Him. All this is possible because Christ Himself, as the Living One, lives in us.*
> — Andrew Murray, Daily Experience with God

People generally do not live their lives accidentally. Every choice they make is a reflection of those things that they love and long for. Those things we worship begin to dictate the way we choose to live our lives. We must be people who live on purpose.

Things happen to us that we cannot control every single day, but the way in which we respond is our own responsibility. Becoming a person who is living out a Gospel-transformed life means that we begin choosing how we will respond to things throughout the various steps of our lives. The Word of God commands us to take control of our thoughts, choosing how we use our words.

As we discussed a few pages back, we either choose to live peaceably with others or not. As it depends on us, we ought to live purposefully for the glory of God. When we have encountered Jesus, it should be evident in the way we live our lives.

ENGAGING ON PURPOSE EVERY DAY

In the book, *Center Church*, Timothy Keller makes the observation that although many of us run from the cities, we as believers should actually be running towards them. He makes the strong case that if God created man in His own image, and we desire to know the image of God, that we should be in the city!

For *"there is more of the image of God per square foot in the city than any other part of the world."*

To begin living on purpose as disciples means that we start to do things differently than either our personal desires or our influencing cultures push us to do.

Our personal desires and tendencies lean toward certain mannerisms and ways of life. Our cultures absolutely push us to conform to certain styles of living, to have particular thought patterns, and to ask questions as society poses them. I would like to examine both of these and find the ways in which we can push back against those influences, becoming more missional in our intent and in our action.

How do we start to make practical choices in our every day life which open the door to share the Gospel?

BUT I'M INTROVERTED

Personalities and preferences differ so vastly that there is no way to cover even a small percentage of them in this book. However, I want to look at the ways a few of our personal desires and tendencies can be intentionally set aside for the sake of the Gospel.

I'm an extroverted person. This is pretty easy to perceive if you've spent any time with me. But a great many of my best friends are introverted, and by God's design we all engage with people differently. It is fantastic. This is so obviously the way we were created by God, and though sometimes we question it, it is in fact flawless.

This portion of the book will not be about how we lean into personality traits to reach people. Instead, hopefully, these thoughts will challenge both the socially-reserved and the outgoing individual alike. I hope that through the lens of the Gospel and the Great Commission imperatives, we may both be stretched to live our lives differently. This must happen so that we might share the reason for the hope that we have.

I couldn't even begin to tell you how many people have told me it must be easier for me to share the Gospel since I have a more naturally outgoing tendency. Be assured, just because I have less inhibition when approaching a stranger doesn't make me a more effective evangelist than God may have created my introverted friends to be.

Some of the most effective Gospel teachers and preachers I know have to withdraw completely from people the moment they finish teaching because they have been so overwhelmed by the experience.

It's ironic how the introvert gets a bad reputation of being withdrawn, excluded from society, and less involved in other people's lives. Meanwhile, the extrovert may be told that they are an overbearing, exhausting individual. We tend to be critical of whatever is opposite of us.

But need I remind you that each of us has been perfectly made? You and I both, regardless of our social spectrums, have not only been created for God's glory, but for His purposes in our communities. **If you have been told that your personality either limits or enables you to be more effective for the Gospel, you have been lied to.** Your personality type is a gift from God and can be used to your advantage as you learn to preach the Gospel in every situation.

Our personality is not a limiting factor of our capacity to share the reason for the hope that we have.

STOP SIGNS

Sometimes what stops us from having the chance to share the Gospel is just what we are doing. Personality aside, think about the stop signs you might be putting up in your life that impede you from having a chance to share Jesus.

I live in a major American city in which I love to work and study out of coffee shops. Sometimes I go out for very specific purposes and with the goal of accomplishing a task. I put in my earbuds and get to work.

Those earbuds are a massive hurdle to the Gospel.

Those earbuds signal to every person sitting near me that I have zero intent of interacting with them. If I am a person looking for every opportunity to share Jesus, then I ought to become hyper-aware in these moments.

Even though I'm intending to accomplish something on my task list, am I putting the brakes on what God might be intending for my time by being unwilling to put down my book and look those around me in the eye to say hello?

Some of my favorite Gospel-focused conversations have happened after the briefest of encounters in places like this. Quick hellos turn into deep conversations if you learn how to guide them there.

A brief greeting and acknowledgment of their existence turns into, "What book is that," "Do you come here often?"

You might explain that you come here before going to church, which turns into you asking, "Did you grow up with a faith of some kind?" Suddenly, you're discussing spiritual things. Now you have a door to share about Jesus.

Become intentional in every moment of your day because you don't know when God is sovereignly causing someone to cross your path.

Take those stop signs out of your ears and engage with the people God puts in your life. You may be only one conversation away from your new best friend. Seek new relationships.

You don't have to be an outrageously extroverted person to ask someone how they are doing. You never know how far that little question will take you. Be ready to engage someone with a real conversation, even when you just want to sit and read by yourself.

To be living on purpose means that you are looking for ways to engage those around you for the sake of the Gospel. It's as simple as that.

CULTURAL INFLUENCES

Our unique societies and micro-cultures are an immense force in our lives, pushing us to live and act in ways that are deemed appropriate or preferred by those around us.

David Platt wrote an entire book on ways that we can live to be *"counter-cultural."* To impart change in the world as disciples, we must live our lives differently than the rest. We are taught in the Bible to live temporarily in this world, but not to conform to it.

How is it that we can live with the pressure of society telling us what to believe and what to worship while refusing to be changed into what the world demands of us?

This is not a task for the faint of heart.

Think about this: every day our local cultures impress upon us what our sexual ethic should be. They tell us how we should think about certain people groups or life-style concepts. Depending on what country you live in, they often limit your expressions of faith. Our cultures impress upon us what families should look like and what objects you ought to purchase to live your very best life.

Every industry that sells something is vying for your affection and worship. They want you to long for their products in such a way that you will entrap yourself in debt to have them. Entire industries are built today to give you the platform for personal expression, which they tell you over and over again is your personal liberty.

Your culture is always waging war against you. It is constantly asking you to conform to its will and thought-process everyday. You must begin to live purposefully, in order to not be swayed by its heavy influence. Find a way to live that resists the forces aiming to distract you from your relationship with Jesus, but interact with them closely so that you have a chance to share Jesus with the countless others swallowed up in its throes.

I urge you once more, the way for you to live on mission in the midst of a culture that is trying to get you to conform to its systems is to stay deeply rooted in the Word of God. When you've become so secure in the truth that the Holy Spirit is guiding your daily choices, you will be able to withstand the temptation to be a relevant part of your local culture.

The only relevancy you need as you go into your community is love. I assure you: love is still relevant in every culture the world around. And **the love that you have to show is a different type of love than they are shouting about on the street corner.**

The version of love the world has for you is a tarnished, broken image of love. It says to love yourself. It tells us that love is love regardless of what genders are involved. Its skewed version of love is so focused on what you and I want, it ignores not only others, but it ignores the very origin of love itself.

You need to realize this: the love that the world says you should have for yourself is not the kind of love that we see anywhere in the Gospel. In fact, I would take this moment to say that when you obey society's demands to forgive yourself, to love yourself, and to practice "self-care" by the world's standards, you are not understanding the Gospel fully. **Self-love is literally an antithesis to the teachings of Jesus.**

I've heard it said this way: "Jesus said to love your neighbor as yourself, because He knows you love yourself plenty already!"

We are told that we should love our neighbor as ourself. A love birthed in the Gospel will prefer others over yourself.

The believer who is firm in their identity in Christ should grow up in maturity to realize that they do not need to forgive themselves. That is the enemy working hard to convince you that you are still guilty. Jesus forgave you already! Walk in that forgiveness.

Self-forgiveness is a form of deceit by the enemy. What good is it to simply forgive yourself if you've not been forgiven by your Creator? Learning to "forgive yourself" as the world says you ought to only creates a shroud of false joy, and even a sense of pride. In your self-forgiveness, you've made the statement that you in fact are capable of erasing the past.

Without an understanding of Jesus' version of forgiveness, you will fall back into a harmful, self-condemning outlook every time you fall short again. Your version of self-care falls far short of God's desire for you to live in freedom. Until you filter that self-forgiveness through the eternal lens of God's forgiveness, you will remain condemned in your own thoughts and feelings. **A disciple of Jesus should lean so hard into their walk with God that the love they have for themselves and others is birthed out of the understanding of the love He has for us.**

Look at how opposite these versions of love are:

- Human culture says to love yourself more.
- Gospel culture tells you to love others more than yourself.

> *Greater love has no one than this, that someone lay down his life for his friends.*
> John 15:13

LIVING OBEDIENTLY

Obedience changes things. In Luke 5, we see Jesus ask Simon to do something very specific. My guess is that it was probably something Simon wouldn't have wanted to do. After a day of hard labor with nothing to show for it, Jesus asked Simon to get back to work. I spent a few years working in a warehouse, so I know a thing or two about labor. I assure you, after eight hours of throwing boxes, the last thing I ever wanted to do at the end of my work day was to go back to work. Knowing that, I am willing to bet that what Jesus was asking of Simon would have been something a worn-out, tired fisherman at the end of his day would not want to do.

The miracle Jesus was about to do happened after Simon obeyed Jesus' request to continue doing what he had already been doing. How many times do we labor all day and get tired of the task, only to miss the miracle because we don't get back to work if Jesus tells us to? The result of Simon's obedience was a catch too big for his boat to even hold. He had to ask others to come assist him with the fruit of his labor. Simon could have said, "I've been working all day, Jesus. I'll throw the nets again tomorrow." Instead, he says in verse five, "Master, we toiled all night and took nothing! But at your word I will let down the nets."

He seems to respond with a moment of doubt, maybe even frustration. **But** he recognized **Who** was giving the command, and so he went back to work. He recognized that when Jesus says to do something, the results will be different than when we labor on our own.

You may be tired. Maybe you are even frustrated at the

lack of fruit coming from your work. From experience, I can say this one thing: obedience changes things. When you have worked all day, do not let your fatigue cause you to ignore (or disobey) the prompting of the Holy Spirit to continue in your labor. You may be only moments away from the biggest catch of your life. **If Jesus says to get back to work, do it.** To live out a Jesus mission means you obey even when you don't feel like it.

RESPONDING TO CHAOS AND DEATH

The reactions we have in moments of confusion, chaos, or even around death can become the greatest opportunity to share the Gospel you may ever have.

When we go through the turbulence of life, the way we showcase the comfort and peace we have in Christ will reveal to those around us that our lives are different than theirs. The way we respond to life's most dreadful events reveals both who we are and who we are are trusting in.

CHAOS

The world seems to be falling apart. Look at any major news publication and you will see that sin is ripping humanity from head to toe. On almost any day of the week now, we see murders, accusations of sexual aggression, scandals, and all kinds of failure. We see this from the highest levels of world leadership to the people living next door. School shootings and violence plague our neighborhoods. Chaos seems to reign supreme.

When we understand that these are the natural results of sin and that the only hope people have for comfort in the midst of chaos is Jesus, we can respond differently. People who understand this and can filter their response to crisis through the hope they have in eternity will be given many chances to give the reason for that hope.

In 1 Peter 3:15, Peter tells the church that even if they suffer for the sake of righteousness, they will be blessed. **Our perspective on chaos and suffering shifts when we know our eternal destiny.**

Suffering causes humanity to see its need for God. While the world groans longingly for the redemption of the Creator, we can use our greatest suffering to assure those around us of our eternal hope. Be ready and willing to give a reason to them for the hope that you have, proving that even in chaos, your hope is in Christ.

DEATH

One of our missionaries in A *Jesus Mission* had a young family member who was violently murdered back home in California while he was deployed on the field. Upon discussion of what he should do, he told me that he intended to stay on the field to continue building the relationships he had been focusing on in the neighborhood he served.

The next day I received an image he sent me of a man's injured foot. The man had his foot damaged in a motorcycle chain years prior, and it had never fully healed. The missionary had gone to help him clean it.

This young man had made the choice to stay behind and wash his neighbor's feet rather than go mourn the death of a family member. His choice was an excellent picture of what it means to count the cost. That only happens when you know the full weight of the message you've gone to declare.

Our outward reactions to death have the opportunity to influence the living.

We do not mourn like the rest of the world, because we have an eternal hope. We have a hope which changes the very approach we have to life. If we can react to death in such a way that we can point people to Jesus through it, then we are effectively living on mission.

When my Dad died of cancer in 2016, we watched many

people who knew our family mourn deeply. While we mourned, we were also taking great joy in the moment, knowing that after the many years of agony and pain he had endured, he had finished the race well. He had his hope set on eternity. He lived his life as a servant to those around him, and he is now in the presence of God. Most certainly he cares not of these things on earth any longer, because he now worships the God of the universe forevermore!

When our sights are on eternity, we celebrate the loss of a believer. While we do mourn the loss and feel the immense sadness of them being gone, we are given the chance to celebrate.

At my Dad's memorial service, there were people who heard the Gospel and responded. It was later told to us that going to his memorial felt more like a church service than a funeral. He would have loved that. We had a chance that day to show people closest to us who don't know Jesus that we handle death much differently.

The way that we respond in moments of chaos or death set us apart from the rest of the world. When we know Jesus, we live differently.

AVOIDING THE APPEARANCE OF EVIL

Growing up in church, I was always told to avoid the appearance of evil. So where does this come from? How do we do this without becoming a slave to what others may (or may not) think of what we are doing?

We don't have to live in fear of what others might think if we are being obedient to the convictions of the Holy Spirit. But we should be careful what we do, what we say, who we spend time alone with, and where we go when we think no one is looking.

We can't be so focused on avoiding what others might think is evil that we run the risk of stepping into the world of legalism. This can cause us to live our lives according to what other people think is "holy" instead of what the Holy Spirit is actually leading us to do. I think it's substantially easier to live a life listening to the Spirit than to live a life attempting to stay within the lines other people are drawing around what is right and wrong.

The verse that people are quoting is 1 Thessalonians 5:22, which says in the NLT, "S*tay away from all kinds of evil.*" Let's think about this for a moment. Isn't that already the job of every person following after Jesus? To turn from evil and do what is good? To repent of sin and strive to be more like Christ?

If you spend your whole life looking at how close to the line of "sinful" you are getting, your focus is on the wrong thing. Remember how spiritually mature people look to Jesus? Keep your eyes there. The line between sinful and righteous is not even something you will need to keep your eye on! If your focus is on Jesus and you're walking towards Him every day, you're going to be keenly aware when the Spirit prompts you to avoid a situation.

We can both guard ourselves and employ wisdom in ways that the Spirit designed. One does not go to war with the flesh without being equipped as a soldier would be. The weapons we have are a bit different from those of the physical battlefield, since our warfare is not against flesh and blood.

> *For our struggle is not against flesh and blood, but against the rulers, against the authorities, against the cosmic powers of this darkness, against evil, spiritual forces in the heavens.*
> *Ephesians 6:12*

PERMISSABLE VS BENEFICIAL

A person living with the conviction of the Spirit may or may not be able to do certain things in their life and remain in obedience.

What the Spirit is convicting you of, you are to obey. What the Spirit convicts your neighbor of is not your responsibility. But if you are aware of their conviction and you knowingly exercise your freedom in Christ in front of them, you are now walking dangerously close to disobedience of the Word.

Paul says that all things are permissible, but that not all things are beneficial (1 Corinthians 10:23). A person living out the mission of Christ recognizes that those in their community will be at varying levels of spiritual maturity. Those of you who are more mature will more often than not have to harness your freedom for the sake of their growth.

Romans 14 addresses this in the area of food and drink. Those who are mature may be able to eat certain meats while

Part Three: Becoming

the one who is not yet free in Christ—through their convictions and understandings of the Word—may only be able to eat vegetables.

Our job is not to judge them, but again, to bear with them. Verse 12 says that each of us will give account of himself to God. Your job is obedience. Listen to the Holy Spirit and live a life reflecting His promptings.

Living on mission means sacrificing preferences, desires, and freedoms for the sake of others so that we may point everybody to Christ.

What things in your life may be permissible, but fall into the category of not being beneficial for those you are serving, loving, or sent to share Jesus with?

PUT ON THE ARMOR

When we go to battle in the spiritual realm, we are not waging a war that can be fought by brute strength and physical capacity. Our stamina to withstand the attacks of the enemy is not found in our own ability. **When we engage in spiritual warfare, we are equipped with the right tools by the Spirit.**

Paul instructs us to *"be strengthened by the Lord and by his vast strength"* (Ephesians 6:10).

Our capacity to stand against the enemy, a pushy cultural environment, and the words of those around us is found in this chapter. If we are to be disciples walking in the fullness of our calling, we will take up this armor because, *"...our struggle* is not against flesh and blood, but against the rulers, against the authorities, against the cosmic powers of this darkness, against evil, spiritual forces in the heavens" (Ephesians 6:12).

Some of you may have learned this in Sunday school. Some of you may have this verse memorized. But I believe it is critical for every person living out the mission of Christ to not only understand the tools we have to engage with, but to employ them. It is wise for us to inventory these armaments every now and then.

> *Stand, therefore, with truth like a belt around your waist, righteousness like armor on your chest, and your feet sandaled with readiness for the gospel of peace. In every situation take up the shield of faith with which you can extinguish all the flaming arrows of the evil one. Take the helmet of salvation and the sword of the Spirit—which is the word of God. Pray at all times in the Spirit with every prayer and request, and stay alert with all perseverance and intercession for all the saints...*
> *Ephesians 6:14-18*

THE BELT OF TRUTH

"Stand, therefore, with truth like a belt around your waist..."
Ephesians 6:14

The belt of truth is the Word of God, the Bible. Paul encourages the person engaged in battle to pick this up and put it on first. Early on in this book, we looked at the authoritative voice by which the Word of God was spoken into being.

No soldier runs into battle without being sent by the leader of the army. And so, we should pick up and know the truth, which is revealed to us in the Word. Stand your ground in the truth. This is your first step to being spiritually guarded against attack.

THE ARMOR OF RIGHTEOUSNESS

"...righteousness like armor on your chest..."
Ephesians 6:14

Note **it is God's righteousness, not yours, that protects you.** No work of holiness is accomplished by you in your own power. It is Him who has done the work of making you holy, through redemption and sanctification.

Put on His righteousness with which to guard your heart and soul. It will withstand much more than your own righteousness is capable of. When we try to build up our own righteousness to repay the debt for our sins, it falls short. But through Jesus' accomplishment on the cross, we are made whole.

Observe what Paul says in his letter to the Romans about the Jews:

> *I can testify about them that they have zeal for God, but not according to knowledge. Since they are ignorant of the righteousness of God and attempted to establish their own righteousness, they have not submitted to God's righteousness. For Christ is the end of the law for righteousness to everyone who believes.*
> *Romans 10:2-4*

They were trying desperately to be right in God's eyes by keeping the law perfectly, but ignoring God's righteousness. It is Christ who makes us right before God! Put on that truth, knowing that your heart is guarded by the accomplishment of Jesus on the cross.

FOR SHOES, PUT ON PEACE

"...and your feet sandaled with readiness for the gospel of peace..."
Ephesians 6:15

We can walk into every battle knowing that our God is fighting for us. It is not a surprise that Paul says we should be fully prepared with the Good News. Putting on the peace that accompanies the Good News will embolden you to walk into situations that would otherwise cause you to tremble.

Where before there was turmoil, we can now walk in absolute peace when we have this news. To put something on means that you actually pick it up, and you put it on! He says that we are to put on that peace, which means you have to choose to put it on. You ought to choose everyday to clad yourself in them.

The Good News gives you boldness to walk into battle. Be prepared and walk boldly in the peace that accompanies your preparation!

THE SHIELD OF FAITH

"In every situation take up the shield of faith with which you can extinguish all the flaming arrows of the evil one…"
Ephesians 6:16

It is through faith that you enter into relationship with Jesus. It is this same faith that protects you from the arrows that the enemy will assuredly launch at you.

Romans 3:28 says, *"We conclude that a person is justified by faith apart from the works of the law."*

Hebrews 11:1-3 says: *"Now faith is the reality of what is hoped for, the proof of what is not seen. For by this our ancestors were approved. By faith we understand that the universe was created by the word of God, so that what is seen was made from things that are not visible."*

These scriptures remind us of this simple truth, that we are justified before God through our faith. Our faith is what gives us an eternal hope and an understanding of how all things came to be. Faith is a mighty force that changes the nature of our relationship with God.

Faith takes our redemption from something based on our works and transforms it into a relational redemption.

In moments of attack from the enemy, lift up that shield and stand firm in faith. I believe there is an incredible power you yield in your words and in your actions when you have this great confidence in Christ. To invoke the name of the One in whom you have faith will quell the ability of the arrows to strike you.

If you feel as though you are being struck by those arrows, remember that we have established that God is working all things together for good. I would assume that Joseph felt as though he was being struck by every arrow that came his way. We know the end of His story; the God in whom he had faith was working that situation out for an eternal purpose. Stand firm.

THE HELMET OF SALVATION

"Take the helmet of salvation..."
Ephesians 6:17

Your mind is where the enemy will wage war against you daily. He has no power to control your thoughts, nor to hear them, but the Bible tells us that satan is the father of lies. We know he is able to speak to us, otherwise we would have no fear of his lies.

I've seen far too many people fall under the pressure of life as they become discouraged and fearful. Don't we stand assured that those of us in Christ have not been given a spirit of fear (Romans 8:15)? Where is all this fear coming from? I believe the enemy is constantly working to lie to us and discourage us.

Satan's most powerful tools are not lust and desire, but often discouragement and defeat.

When we know that our salvation is sure, we are more confident throughout the battle. It is no surprise Paul references the assurance of salvation as something to secure our mind behind. Put on the helmet of salvation! Have your mind be guarded by that future hope!

When you begin to entertain doubts of your salvation, take them captive and subject them to the truth you know of the Gospel. We are told we have the capacity to do this in 2 Corinthians 10, where Paul is addressing the topic of spiritual warfare:

> *Since the weapons of our warfare are not of the flesh, but are powerful through God for the demolition of strongholds. We demolish arguments and every proud thing that is raised up against the knowledge of God, and we take every thought captive to obey Christ.*
> *2 Corinthians 10:4-5*

I love that he says we are to be casting down arguments, and also bringing every thought into captivity.

The Greek word he uses for captivity is rooted in the word for "to capture." We are to grab hold of them, arrest them, and subject them to the truth we know in Christ! Do this forcefully and with authority, because your mind is guarded by the helmet of salvation. Of this you can stand assured.

THE SWORD OF THE SPIRIT

> "...the sword of the Spirit—which is the word of God..."
> Ephesians 6:17

This one should not require much explication. The weapon we fight spiritual warfare with is the truth of the Word of God in its exact form. We do not need to enhance it nor parse it down.

We need to know it. It is in knowing the Word that we can wield it as a sword. We know from scripture that the Spirit bears the truth of God to mind, so our job is to know the Word so the Spirit can bear it as a blade at the right time.

> *For the word of God is living and effective and sharper than any double-edged sword, penetrating as far as the*

> *separation of soul and spirit, joints and marrow. It is able to judge the thoughts and intentions of the heart.*
> *Hebrews 4:12*

This is a challenging verse, because God knows the condition of our heart and the truth the Word holds will confront us in our sin. We must let the Word of God confront and split our own sinful nature so that you can yield it as a sword in moments of attack.

It is a powerful truth that we hold in our hands when we pick up the Bible. With it we stand and resist the enemy, but we also allow it to cut us to the bone so that we may be right before God. Bear the Word of God well, that you may live on mission with great authority.

PRAY IN THE SPIRIT

"Pray at all times in the Spirit with every prayer and request, and stay alert with all perseverance and intercession for all the saints."
Ephesians 6:18

Here we are told once again to pray at every occasion, not only for ourselves but for other believers who are also waging war against the powers of this world. We do fight a spiritual battle, and as we lift each other up in prayer we are in obedience to the command of the Gospel.

No piece of this armor should be ignored as we live as missionaries in our cities. We need the protection and confidence of the Word of God and the assurance of our salvation. We need peace to accompany us as we walk in faith.

Part Three: Becoming

YOU CAN'T CONTROL WHAT OTHERS SAY

As we aim to avoid evil in our lives as Paul instructed the Church to do, we will be making a lot of hard choices. As we discussed earlier, some of those choices may be the sacrifice of our personal liberties. But isn't the opportunity to point someone to Jesus worth far more than a glass of wine with dinner? Sometimes, for the sake of the Gospel, and when prompted by the Spirit, you may need to sacrifice that. Other-times however, you may need to realize your legalistic tendencies could be hindering a chance to share the Gospel, and be comfortable with being uncomfortable.

As my band traveled for more than a decade, we learned

some pretty hard truths that confronted us in bizarre ways. I can't tell you how many times we instantly felt regret for something we did or said as we lived on mission, stayed in peoples homes, went to new cities, and stood on stage to tell people about Jesus. It came down to us learning how to be hyper-intentional in everything we said and did. This intentionality could have been the difference between our invitation back to perform another time or them choosing not to contact us again.

We learned this valuable lesson: **you can't control what others say, but you can control what they see.**

This phrase became something of a motto for us, reminding us to be overly intentional in all things. As we went on mission as a band, we made sure to talk to as many people as we could. Our group intentionally sat at different tables at meals so that we could collectively engage with as many people as possible wherever we were.

In an age where accusation is enough to destroy people's lives, we should be aiming to avoid the appearance of evil. We should be very careful that the things we say or do in public or in private are honoring of God and others.

But a Christian who is living under the influence of the Spirit of God does not need to live in fear if they are listening and obeying. The Spirit will prompt you when it's time to avoid a situation. He will convict you if the action you are doing is a sinful one.

When you read the Psalms, you see the writer constantly speak as though many enemies are waging war against him through their words and with their actions. As he cries out to God, he becomes assured over and over again that even though many are against Him, the Almighty God is for Him.

When many war against you, walk in the wisdom of the Spirit and act according to His prompting. By doing so, you will be living in a manner that is sensitive to situations, yet confidently acting when it is required.

Work to control what others see, so they may have nothing but good to say.

Part Three: Becoming

THE IMPORTANCE OF REALLY GOOD RELATIONSHIPS

As my band traveled as missionaries and musicians with a purpose, we had to learn fast how to maintain and grow God-honoring relationships.

So many little things war against our interpersonal relationships every single day: money, stress, jealousy, anger, and fear. All of these are things that can impede the growth of relationships as we live on mission.

We have to be guarded against these temporal things interfering in relationships that have eternal impact. We need to be slow to speak and quick to listen with each other. We should be seeking healthy friendships and relationships because those are a reflection of the Gospel being lived out in our lives.

We don't do this just to create a healthy workplace or long-lasting friendships. We do this because it is an imperative from the word of God! If you have weak relationships, strengthen them. If you have great relationships, maintain them!

Spend time with people, both inside and outside of your direct circle of influence and friendship. Look for new people to begin relationships with. Do things with people. Invite them into your home. Go to their home. Do Kingdom work together with believers. Sacrifice your personal time to spend it with other people for the sake of sharing the Gospel.

Be in healthy relationships with people!

BECOMING RECONCILERS

Restoring brokenness is often the hardest part of maintaining healthy relationships. I've been married since I was 19, so I have had to learn how to maintain and reconcile every day. Marriage is an awesome place to work out living in unity because it is an example of Christ and the Church. Relationships that build depth effectively reveal how the Gospel works in us.

We are to be known for reconciling people and relationships. People who are doing Jesus' mission need to understand this crucial piece of our role in the mission.

Our friendships and closest relationships should be the living examples of our willingness to be reconcilers. Reconciliation in action means that we are restoring broken relationships. To reconcile something means it is being repaired.

Too many times we are willing to let friendships have relational distances that are caused by momentary arguments with literally **no** eternal impact. Why on earth do we let things with zero eternal substance destroy our ability to communicate things of eternal importance with people?

Money, preferences, opinions, and methodologies should never be things we allow to impede our ability to share who Jesus is. If something is broken and we have the capacity to restore it, we should be actively seeking its restoration.

As believers, we draw our understanding of reconciliation from the very nature of God Himself. The Gospel in itself is a reconciling equation! The entire point of the Gospel is to restore the broken relationship that humanity has with its Creator. If we are doing Jesus' mission, we will be seeking the restoration of people, period.

Paul hits on this often, but for this chapter I'm just going to draw from 1 Corinthians 5. We are being told by Paul that those who understand the good news have been given the ministry of reconciliation. If we skip this part, we've missed the whole point.

Part Three: Becoming

THE LOVE OF CHRIST COMPELS US

> *"For the love of Christ compels us, since we have reached this conclusion, that one died for all, and therefore all died. And he died for all so that those who live should no longer live for themselves, but for the one who died for them and was raised. From now on, then, we do not know anyone from a worldly perspective. Even if we have known Christ from a worldly perspective, yet now we no longer know him in this way. Therefore, if anyone is in Christ, he is a new creation; the old has passed away, and see, the new has come! Everything is from God, who has reconciled us to himself through Christ and has given us the ministry of reconciliation. That is, in Christ, God was reconciling the world to himself, not counting their trespasses against them, and he has committed the message of reconciliation to us. Therefore, we are ambassadors for Christ, since God is making his appeal through us. We plead on Christ's behalf, "Be reconciled to God.""*
> 2 Corinthians 5:14-20

Re-read this part: *"The love of Christ compels us!"*

Love is our driving factor. Nothing should motivate us more than our understanding of the love of Christ. It changes lives. It changes **us**! And so, love in itself should motivate our engagement in the mission.

God, in His grace and nature, saw fit to restore us into right relationship with Himself through Jesus. Paul makes the case in the verses above that we, who have been restored, have now been given the very task of restoration. Don't be mistaken, it is not that we have any ability to restore anyone to God in ourselves, but rather we have the understanding and the key to that restoration. His name is Jesus.

The name of Jesus is in our possession, and we who understand its power need to be making His name known to those who don't yet know. If we are compelled by the love of Christ, then doing a Jesus mission means that, through love, we will constantly be aiming for the restoration of people to God.

We can (and must) begin doing this in our own lives immediately. Too many of us who boldly claim that our lives have been transformed by the Gospel have broken relationships with those who are (or were) close to us. We have broken trust. We have broken families. We have sin.

If we are unable to forgive as Christ forgave, then we will be hindered in our undertaking of the mission. **Our own lives are no longer declaring that we are free in Christ, because we voluntarily submit ourselves to the chains of un-forgiveness.** Our prime example of forgiveness is Jesus on the cross. He literally forgave as they were in the act of crucifying

Part Three: Becoming

him (Luke 23:34). Every moment we hold on to anger towards someone without forgiving them is a moment we are walking in sin.

We cannot reconcile others to God until we recognize and respond to the reconciliation that has occurred on our behalf. That understanding of Christ's love should compel us to repair those broken things.

Where do we start?

We start with those closest to us. We cannot effectively engage in the mission of Christ without restoring those broken relationships. Probably, as you read the previous paragraphs, somebody came to mind. I would challenge you to put down this book, pray for the heart of God in that relationship, and go seek restoration. Start with the family member who you had an argument with. Start with your spouse. Start with your children. Start with your neighbor or your co-worker. Just pick any of the broken relationships in your life and go seek its reconciliation.

Take it from me, I know this from personal experience. I would predict that seeking to reconcile will create an opportunity for you to share why you are making that specific effort. Now, suddenly, by actively aiming to restore a human relationship, you will have an open door to point that person toward the restoration of their eternal relationship.

We have, according to this text, been given the ministry of restoration. At the most basic level of what it means to be doing Jesus' mission, we are to be seeking and restoring relationships.

God was, **in Christ**, reconciling the world to Himself. The portal of restoration to Him came through the cross. He took the penalty for sin so that those who believe would not be held to the burden of paying the price for their own sins. Paul says that God has committed to **us** the work of reconciliation. **People who are are engaged in the mission of Christ are reconcilers.**

Part Three: Becoming

THE IMPORTANCE OF BEING A PART OF THE CHURCH

Living out your faith, long-term, without being engaged in a healthy church body is possible. You can have a relationship with Jesus that is not associated with a local body of believers. Be warned, however, you will not grow as God intended. Also, you will miss out on the astounding joy that comes along with living as God desires, in close relationships with Himself and others.

Jesus maintained close proximity with His disciples and taught them to remain and minister together.

> *Let us consider one another in order to provoke love and good works, not neglecting to gather together, as some are in the habit of doing, but encouraging each other, and all the more as you see the day approaching.*
> Hebrews 10:24-25

Paul directly tells the Church to gather. Clearly, some were choosing to stop gathering and he calls them out on it. We are to be meeting together and exhorting one another, pushing each other towards love and good works, more so now than ever before. We do this urgently because we know the day is approaching in which Jesus will return.

It seems more so in recent years that I have heard far too may Christians begin to justify their pulling away from the local body. Modern technologies have created the opportunity for people to be a "part" of church while abstaining from actual community. Churches are giving people an easy out, and I fear it will harm the Body over time.

Hear me out on this. I do not think that churches should stop streaming services and limit the hearing of the Gospel to when it is only happening in person. There is much use for the digital distribution of the Word of God, both in written and spoken form.

My mother is restricted in her movement and travel ability because of her health, so she uses the streaming of services as a way to hear the preaching of the Word every week. This is a wonderful help to those who are limited in some way.

But let's be absolutely clear: hearing the Word of God and singing together is only a small portion of the work of the Church on Sunday morning. In the book of Acts we see the Church established, then entire communities of people changed the way that they lived their lives. Being a part of the Church is about letting the Gospel challenge and confront your sin together and living outwardly to impact your city with the same news that has changed you.

The Gospel should impact you in such a way that it drives you **toward** community, not away from it.

I've heard far too many of my own friends give lengthy arguments for their disassociation from church. They have been burned by people within its walls. Their kids were not getting what they had hoped from the children's ministry. The style of the music has changed and they no longer felt drawn into worship. The teacher taught something that offended them.

Every one of these reasons is about them and not about the body of Christ. Church is not intended to be your favorite environment of the week, where you are perfectly satisfied by the sounds, smells, and sights.

There are obvious exceptions to this statement, such as abusive or physically unhealthy leadership, false teachings, or other things of that nature. If you are not being taught the Word of God as the absolute authority in your Christian walk, then it is not a church that is making disciples.

What I am talking about is those moments when the Gospel is being taught, and it is confronting your sin, but you are choosing to elevate your preference or concept of church over the top of it. If you are in a church that is not pointing you to Jesus, then you are probably in a church that is not operating under God's intended design.

I've listened to many people give reasons for their abstaining from church. Rarely have I heard reasons that merit an actual departure from the body. Around 90% of the time, it is for reasons of preference or relational friction.

I urge you—if you have withdrawn from a church for any reason other than false teaching or abuse—to submit your relational friction to the commands of the Word. Submit your preferences to the confrontation of the Word and make sure you are listening to the voice of the Spirit. I would argue that He will likely convict you of your sin and urge you back into the community God has designed.

If you are feeling disconnected, it's probably because you are not plugged in. To be connected requires literal points of connection.

A lot of people have told me over the years that they didn't feel connected in their church. Their reasons normally are that it is either too big or too small. It has either no room for them to plug into an activity or it's too big to plug into.

Being plugged into a church is less about the tasks you're doing and more about the relationships you're a part of. By serving the Body in a task-driven way, you are submitting your time and you are worshiping God through your undertakings. By building relationships within the Body, you are allowing God to grow you in spiritual maturity.

Get off the bench and get in the game. Stop making excuses. If you don't have a local church, find one that is teaching the Bible and submit to the refining nature of God that occurs when people are learning together. Being in church matters because we are called to be the Church together every day. It is for the edification of the whole body that you join in and use your gifting to push the mission forward.

If you are living overseas or in a place where there is no local church body, perhaps that is why you are there. Maybe you are there on mission by God's design to be working to draw believers together for a regular gathering in which you allow the Spirit to lead everyone into deeper relationship. Be the Church where you are.

> *They devoted themselves to the apostles' teaching, to the fellowship, to the breaking of bread, and to prayer.*
> Acts 2:42

The early Church met together as they grew. As you continue engaging in the mission today, you need to continue as instructed. Be actively involved in the Body of Christ. It is for all of our benefit.

Part Three: Becoming

WHAT IS THE RIGHT KIND OF CHURCH?

There isn't one.

As it turns out, God's perfect design of the Church didn't mandate we gather in any specific way, day, or place. Rather, I would argue that every gathering of the people of God constitutes a visible expression of the Church.

Our job is to be the Church, not to go to church.

Yes, I emphasized earlier that you need to be a part of the local church. Yes, it is vital that you be plugged into a community of believers focused on growing in spiritual maturity and letting the Spirit operate within your midst. Yes, you need to carve out time in your week to intentionally live alongside other believers who will push you into greater depths.

However, there is no "right kind of church."

Think about this with me. There are more forms of the Church globally than could even be listed within this book's cover. There are churches that gather in elegant buildings and some that meet in bars. Some of them gather in homes while others gather in driveways.

Many of them cannot gather at all. But does that stop them? No. Some of them have to meet in basements with blacked out windows while others meet behind stained glass.

Regardless of its many forms, the Church has been meeting together for thousands of years. And we will continue until the return of Christ.

What we must be careful of, however, is our intrinsic nature to be critical of anything opposite our preferred method. The Gospel demands that we meet together. We must not cease. Despite the many forms of the Church, we must remember that the Spirit is in fact guiding the Church.

Though you may prefer a building you walk into on Sunday, there may be portions of the Church gathering in a basement on the other side of town. You will interpret portions of scripture differently and choose different songs. You will find growth accompanies your Christian community as you undertake various tasks and strategies together.

Your preference doesn't mean the church on the other side of town is failing at the mission God has called them to. **Our Mission in Christ is to be obedient, to grow together, and to live as the Church on mission in every context known to man.** Read the Word of God and respond to it. Sing songs together. Pray together. Exercise the gifts together. Push each other back to Jesus every time you fail, and be obedient to what God is convicting your church to do. As long as the mission hasn't changed, neither has our commission.

To change the world, the Church must continue being the Church. Don't stop gathering.

Part Three: Becoming

BUILD RELATIONSHIPS THAT CAUSE YOU TO GROW

I read once that our personalities are the average of the five people we spend the most time with, which actually makes a lot of sense to me. Having traveled in a band for years in extremely close proximity with the same three to five people, I realize that I now laugh at the things that my band members found funny. My personality and character have been directly influenced by them. In some ways for the better, in other ways at a cost.

To my great joy, those people who were easygoing caused me to become more relaxed. Those people who traveled with us who could make light of a difficult situation helped me to do the same. Adversely, those people in that circle who were quick to anger caused me to become more angry. Those people who were passive-aggressive built a tendency in me to be the same way. We do become like those people we surround ourselves with.

Earlier we looked at how our cultures are pushing us to act or become something we are not. The micro-cultures of our friend groups are doing the same thing.

Yes, we are supposed to engage the lost and interact with them so that we might win them to Christ. But with those people who you allow to influence you directly, be very wise in choosing them. I do believe you should choose them, and do this shamelessly! There are times when I have told people directly that I wanted to be around them, because I wanted to become more like them!

We should find people to disciple, but we should also find people to disciple us. Intentionally seeking out people that will challenge your personality and your spiritual depth to greater levels will be one of the best decisions you can ever make.

If we are to live effectively on mission, we need to find people who will spur us on to good works and challenge us to make the changes in our character that need to be made.

The Word of God confronts our natures and traits, but our direct influences can encourage us to live either for ourselves or for eternity. Choose ones who will do the latter.

LEARNING ON PURPOSE

Traveling often, I found that the circle of influence on my life was sometimes limited. This limitation was not always bad, though, because I believe God brought the right people into our traveling ministry and into our lives for the correct season we were in. But I wanted to purposefully subject myself to even greater potential of growth.

It has been said by many, "*If you are the smartest person in the room, then find a different room.*"

Hear me when I say, I don't know that I have ever been the smartest person in the room in my life. I am drawing this saying to your attention to highlight the way we should be challenged to seek out wisdom that surpasses our own.

Solomon asked for wisdom when he was given the chance to ask God for whatever he wished. He understood that greater wisdom was of more value than riches.

We can scour Proverbs and learn a wealth of wisdom. We can examine history to see what wise choices should have been made in hindsight. And we can invite people, who are educated in areas we are not, to be a part of our life.

I want to encourage you not only to seek people who can push you to greater depth, but to seek and gain knowledge.

Read a lot. Read books outside your normal area of focus. Look for books on topics you are interested in. Seek knowledge and perspective from those who have gone through things you've never experienced. God gave us the capacity to create words and pass those on throughout generations. He gave us His written Word, which is a marvel in itself! Don't miss the chance to learn from others.

I choose to read a lot because I know my circle of influence is sometimes limited when I travel. I challenge you to look for influences in your own life that challenge you to grow, both in depth of knowledge and in maturity. Your growth in an area of knowledge may give you the tools you need to present the Gospel in unique situations later.

Continued education may open broader doors for you to speak authoritatively in an area that no other believer is speaking to.

Part Three: Becoming

STAYING HEALTHY

As people sent on mission, we must understand this from the start: **those who willfully choose to go on mission are charging headfirst toward an onslaught of attack in both the physical and the spiritual realm.**

The enemy we face absolutely will not stop. He cannot stop. His very nature is destruction. His focus is the pursuit of, the distraction of, and the destruction of God's chosen people. As we have said already, his default method of attack is to lie to us. He aims to make attempts at diminishing Kingdom pursuits through the discouragement and disqualification of those who step out in faith to make the Gospel known.

For people who respond to the Gospel and make a choice

to go on mission, **these two things will ensure longevity: a healthy prayer life and a right perspective.**

Equipped with these two things, we will have the endurance we need to withstand even the enemy's most vicious attacks. His greatest lies are easily overlooked when our perspective is on the victory of the cross and the surety of God's promises to His children.

Having a correct perspective will keep our focus on the end goal. We maintain this understanding by knowing the truth of God's written Word and by recognizing that our identity is secured in Jesus. We must realize that our identity is not in our failures, nor our seemingly disqualifying attributes. Devour the written Word of God, and know the truths inside of it. **Live your life as a believer through the lens of the cross rather than the words of a liar.**

As we align our perspective on eternity and with correct understanding, the end goal will stay correctly in focus as we do the mission of Christ. "*Set your mind on things that are above, not on things that are on earth. For you have died, and your life is hidden with Christ in God*" (Colossians 3:2-3).

Endless prayer will sustain us through both our darkest moments and our greatest victories.

Our access to God through prayer is an embarrassingly untapped resource in most people's Christian walk. Paul emphasizes this vital spiritual discipline in his letter to the Thessalonians saying, "*Rejoice always, pray without ceasing,* give thanks in all circumstances; for this is the will of God in Christ Jesus for you" (1 Thessalonians 5:16-18).

A healthy, constant prayer life will give us the communicative substance in our relationship with God that will give us both the clarity of our calling and the endurance in the shadows.

Keep your perspective right and your prayer life constant.

Also, don't forget to rest. If you are to stay healthy as you live out the Gospel, you need to be obedient to the example and commands of Jesus. In the creation of the earth, God set the example for us by resting on the seventh day.

He did good work as He created the earth and all it holds. But He also stopped for a time. I've been involved in ministry of some kind since I was 15 years old. At the time of writing this, I have been learning the absolute need for rest in the life of a person on mission.

I've had to learn over the course of my life this highly costly lesson: **constant activity doesn't necessarily equate to constant ministry.** In my twenties, I was invincible. I could stay moving and ministering all day every day for months on end. We learned to "rest" as we would travel, which for most people is an exhausting task in itself. It was an adaptive form of rest, not real rest.

Now, as I've aged a few years, I've learned that I need real rest in order to keep my focus on the long game. Real rest needs to include the departure of my mind from the tasks that continue day in and day out. We don't live in a time in which that is easy for us.

People expect replies to be instant. Technology has taken away the luxury of a reply. We become frustrated if a reply to our communique takes more than a moment. It has damaged our capacity to actually rest, because we feel the pressure to reply to everything instantly.

Many books and self-help advisors have suggested what those of us looking at God's example already know: putting everything aside for a time is vital for our emotional and physical health.

I would encourage you to examine how you rest if you desire to stay healthy as you live on mission. God's design was for man to take a break. He created the concept for us, not that we do it because it is in the rules, but because He knows us. He created us. He created the Sabbath for us, so we ought to rest in Him.

> *Then he told them, "The Sabbath was made for man and not man for the Sabbath. So then, the Son of Man is Lord even of the Sabbath."*
> *Mark 2:27-28*

Staying healthy as you live on mission not only sets an example for those who are lost by showing them who your Sustainer is, but enables you to continue reaching the lost for a lifetime.

DOING THE WORD

> But be doers of the word and not hearers only, deceiving yourselves. Because if anyone is a hearer of the word and not a doer, he is like someone looking at his own face in a mirror. For he looks at himself, goes away, and immediately forgets what kind of person he was. But the one who looks intently into the perfect law of freedom and perseveres in it, and is not a forgetful hearer but a doer who works—this person will be blessed in what he does.
> James 1:22-25

Part Three: Becoming

Not much needs to be said after those clear words. If we expect to see results as we engage in the work, we need to be people who not only know the Word but are doing it. We need to be actually living it out in our daily lives. Action follows our beliefs.

We all know somebody who has read a hundred books on a topic and talks about it all the time. They're the person that tells everybody else what they are doing wrong when they see it being done, and yet have never done the very thing they are talking about.

Don't be the type of person that James is writing about. When you hear the Word, put it into action today! Don't spend a week thinking about it, but get to it! When the Word says to act, act. When it says to keep your words, stay silent. People who want to see the Word of God come to life will live it out when they have the chance. The Word of God lives inside you as you do it.

Read the Word, know the Word, and feast on it when you are starving for comfort or truth. Do what it says!

GOING INTO THE WORLD

You may be called to go far, to go into parts of the world that others may never see. If you have that calling and desire, then I urge you to obey. Luke 10:2 says that we are to be praying for workers to be raised up, because the harvest is ready! I make it a point to pray that prayer every single day, because I have such a desire and hope to see people step into the work of global evangelism and mission.

But, I also am praying that prayer for those of you who may never get on a plane in your life. The harvest is ready in your home. The harvest is ready in your high school. The harvest is ready in your workplace. The harvest is waiting to be brought in, and you and I are those whom have been called to do the work.

The reason I'm investing hours into writing this book is because my heart breaks at the idea that so few believers are living out the mission of Christ. Far too many people are dying and going to hell while believers are standing idly by.

Many of you feel under-equipped for the task. Many of you might not realize the call is for you. Many of you are afraid.

Please take these words of encouragement as a push towards living a drastically missional life. There is a great joy to be had for those who give up their lives for the sake of Christ.

Some of you are called to fund those who go. Many have been blessed for the sake of blessing others, which only serves to bring more glory to God!

Some of you are set apart for the work of ministry in a local church, serving the body in ways that utilize gifts and capacities that no other person has.

Please, won't you join in the mission? Won't you stand up from your seat and engage in the work alongside Jesus, who has sent you to do just that?

We go into the world on a mission because we are sent.

DON'T MISS THE POINT

I've missed the mark on this next part too many times. It's so easy to do, though. For those on the mission field or in ministry of some sort, we launch out with good intentions as we look for a way to share the Gospel with people. We spend hours developing a talent, building a plan, raising funds, or doing the task of evangelism.

In my own life, I've noticed it is too easy for us to elevate the task itself above the purpose.

We become so focused on the method that we lose sight of the mission.

Without the eternal perspective of Christ's mission, we end up being people doing various things to fill our time, no matter how well-intended it is. If we spend all of our time preparing for the opportunity to share the Gospel but fall short of sharing the true hope of Jesus, we have missed the whole point.

A number of years ago, I was convicted of the fact that our band was really great at sharing the Gospel and proclaiming the Good News aloud, but we rarely gave people the chance to respond to it.

To be honest, I was afraid.

What if nobody responded?

What if it offended the venue and we weren't invited back?

What if we were only going half way?

What if, what if…

To share the Gospel and stop there is to not fully understand the command we've been given. We've stopped just short of completion.

We're supposed to go into the world and preach the Gospel, teaching them all that He's commanded us, right? He has commanded that we confess our sins. He commanded that we go from unbelief to belief. We need to see it through to completion whenever possible!

I was convicted that, though we were really good at sharing the Gospel, we were not always inviting people into the next step of accepting Christ as their Savior. We, to some degree, were elevating the method over the mission. All of our best intentions were being executed. We were refining our skills and building relationships that enabled us to keep going and play shows, but we weren't always inviting people to follow Jesus.

So we changed the plan. If we were ever sharing the Gospel, either to a single person or to a massive crowd, we would include the invitation to respond. And, just like that, people responded. Yes, some rejected the truth we were proclaiming, but more often than not people eagerly received the Gospel and admitted their need for Jesus.

The mission demands that we invite people to respond.

As we became emboldened to invite people into a response, we saw literally hundreds and thousands of people begin to confess their need for Christ. People were deciding to follow Jesus! When we put the mission over the method, people responded.

If you are phenomenal at loving people but are not expressing why you are driven to do so, you're stopping short. If you focus on a talent and hope that it will give you the chance to have a later conversation, you're missing the opportunity.

DOING WHAT YOU LOVE

We learned how to use music as a means to open the door to conversation so that we could share Jesus. To me, it was only ever a tool to be used for that purpose. I've never been a fantastic musician, nor one who wants to sit around writing songs for hours. It was just something I knew how to do, and we set to work to do it with a purpose.

Honestly, outside of that I never seemed to have another plan. I really enjoy watching political movies and reading about politics. Maybe I would have aimed to be a politician if I was starting over. I also really love to fly. Maybe I would have been a pilot.

What I want you to realize is that while some may have a larger audience to teach Jesus than others, we all have a sphere of influence in which the Lord has placed us.

Do the mission there.

If you are a parent teaching your children all that He has commanded us, you are just as successfully living out the mission of Christ as a missionary. Your job is to be obedient where God has placed you and to listen to the voice of the Spirit as you live out your life.

Gospel work is not solely for the vocational minister or the overseas missionary. It is for every one of us who has been transformed by the person of Jesus. Our job is to equip the found and to find the lost.

BECOMING PEOPLE WHO WILL CHANGE THE WORLD

Our mission in Christ has not changed since the day He invoked it of us. **There is no mission more vital for all of humanity than Gospel declaration.**

I've named this book specifically *Our Mission In Christ: Becoming People Who Will Change The World*.

I truly believe that if we understand the mission more clearly, prepare for it adequately, and surround ourselves with others who will push us towards it, then we will see people's lives changed drastically as we undertake this task together.

Becoming people who will change the world is about more than becoming the most proficient human being with your specific skillset. It doesn't mean that you are enacting radical social measures to accomplish world peace. It doesn't mean you are writing books that influence millions. It doesn't mean you're even going to be known by the world for any-thing in particular.

It does mean that, every single day you are alive, you're taking intentional actions that are pointing people to know the person of Jesus.

Jesus changes lives, and for some strange reason He completes the mission through us as we live alongside each other. In this we will begin to see the world transformed.

Let all of us who have been saved live on a Jesus mission every single day. That is how we will become people who will change the world.